CIA WIFE

CIA WIFE

One Woman's Life
Inside the CIA

FLORENCE FITZSIMMONS GARBLER

Fithian Press
SANTA BARBARA • 1994

Design and typography by Jim Cook

Published by Fithian Press
Post Office Box 1525
Santa Barbara, California 93102

LIBRARY OF CONGRESS CATALOGING-IN-PUBLICATION DATA
Fitzsimmons Garbler, Florence
    CIA wife: one woman's life inside the CIA / Florence Fitzsimmons
Garbler.
        p. cm.
    ISBN 1-56474-089-7
    1. Garbler, Paul   2. Fitzsimmons Garbler, Florence
3. Garbler, Paul   4. Intelligence agents' spouses—United States
—Biography. 5. United States. Central Intelligence Agency—Biography.
I. Title.
E840.8.G34F58   1994
973.91´092—dc20
[B]   93-39322
                                                          CIP

For Susan

Contents

"AND YE SHALL KNOW THE TRUTH AND
THE TRUTH SHALL MAKE YOU FREE."

—Gospel of St. John, Chapter 8, Verse 32

*Inscribed in marble at the main entrance
to CIA Headquarters in Langley, Virginia.*

1. Tucson

I WAS DOWN at the bottom of a deep, dark well, struggling to get out. Each time I thought I could fight my way to the top, where the daylight was, I seemed to slide back into darkness. Finally I broke through, and there was daylight all around me. Out of the haze came a strange face, attached to a slim body in a blue operating-room scrub suit. Behind the nurse I could make out the concerned faces of my husband, Paul, and my daughter Susan.

I had just been wheeled into the intensive care unit of the El Dorado Hospital in Tucson after four hours of open-heart surgery. There was a breathing tube in my throat that reached down into my lungs and was attached to a large respirator machine that stood by the side of the bed. That tube became my most hated enemy as I lay flat on my back for four days, my hands held in restraints at the side of the bed so that I would not be able to tear out the tube. Paul was there when the doctors removed the tube, and I remember I saw tears in his eyes as he watched it emerge.

Recovery from the trauma of surgery took much longer than the doctors wanted. I made several detours along the way. One morning about two weeks after the surgery, I found myself in a tastefully furnished, sun-splashed hospital room, sitting up in bed, going through the local newspaper. Depression is a common post-heart surgery syndrome, and I had had my share of it, tears coming often to my eyes against my will. But this morning was different.

This morning I knew I was going to make it, I would recover. It was the first baby step on the road I would travel to return to good health.

Tired of reading, I put the newspaper aside to lie back and reflect on what a wonderful life I'd shared with Paul and the years that we still had before us to enjoy. Whether you like it or not, open-heart surgery gives you pause. You think about the kind of things that do not normally come to mind. Like dying, for example, and not wanting to go just yet. So I let my mind drift pleasantly back over what it had been like for Paul and me for forty-nine years of married life.

Being married for forty-nine years makes Paul and me sound a bit dull. But our life together has been anything but dull. There were new countries to visit every few years, new nationalities to get to know, new challenges to meet, new crises to cope with. We spent nineteen of Paul's twenty-six years with the Central Intelligence Agency in postings abroad. During that time, we lived in twenty-one different homes. I was constantly scrambling to keep up, and none of that was dull, I assure you.

2. Jacksonville

MY STORY begins on a hot, sticky day in Jacksonville, Florida, in June 1942. Together with four other Army nurses, I had come to the city from nearby Camp Blanding for some last-minute shopping. We were part of a field hospital unit that had been formed a year earlier at Roosevelt Hospital in New York City. We had survived the training that was meant to make us more "regulation," and now we were itching to get overseas.

Unit gossip had it that we would be shipping out soon, first to North Africa and then to Italy, where the action was. I had been trained as an operating room supervisor. More than anything else, I wanted to be close to combat, caring for the wounded, helping any way I could. And I desperately wanted to get out there before the war was over. I thought of it as the biggest adventure of my life, and I didn't want it to evaporate before I could get to it. I admit I was a bit starry-eyed about it all, but that's the kind of war it was. It was the last "good" war America was to fight until Desert Storm.

We wanted to be certain we had everything females need to survive, and we had plodded through one store after another. Leg-weary, we sought out a cool oasis where we could rest until the bus picked us up for our return to camp. The Roosevelt Hotel had the only air-cooled bar in town, and that's where we were resting our weary feet.

Florence with patients at Camp Blanding (1942).

We had just received our drinks when three young naval officers entered and ordered drinks at the bar. Two wore single ensigns' stripes on their shoulder boards, and the bar lights glanced off them. They also wore shiny gold wings on their left breasts. The third had only a gold star on his shoulder boards and wore no wings. One of the ensigns was tall and slim, with close-cropped dark hair. The other was a bit heavier, with reddish curly hair and the map of Ireland drawn across his face. The cadet was shorter than the other two and looked to be a bit on the pudgy side.

From where we sat, we could see that the three men at the bar were engaged in animated conversation, the ensigns gesturing toward our table and the cadet shaking his head. Finally, the ensigns took the cadet by the arms and propelled him toward where we sat pretending we had no interest whatsoever in what they were doing. When he stood before us, cap in hand, the cadet said in a low voice we could barely hear, "My friends at the bar got their commissions and wings yesterday. They want to know if you'll join them for dinner so they can celebrate."

My roommate Alice, a long-stemmed blonde Texas girl who was anything but shy, spoke up first:

"You mean all of us? All five?"

"Yup, they're loaded. They got a lot of back pay yesterday.

And they wanted me to tell you they're not prejudiced against the Army."

"Big deal," Alice retorted. "You can tell your two bashful buddies we'll be delighted to join them for dinner if they can provide us with transportation back to Camp Blanding. Our bus leaves in forty-five minutes."

The cadet seemed relieved that we were going to make life easier for him, and the two brand-new officers, apparently drunk with power, might get off his back. So he turned toward the bar and gave them the thumbs-up sign. Drinks in hand, and with what I'm sure were meant to be winning smiles, they sauntered over to our table.

The dark-haired ensign seated himself between Alice and me. His companion found a chair at the other end of the table. They introduced themselves as Bill Green and Paul Garbler. The cadet seated himself somewhere between the ensigns, but a bit away from the table, as if to make us think he wasn't really there.

Florence (second from right) with nurses at Camp Blanding (1942).

13

As soon as all the shifting of chairs was completed, Paul raised his glass and said, "Ladies, we hope you will forgive us for forcing our company on you this way. But we wanted to drink to you Florence Nightingales and wish you the best, wherever you go. We hope your patients will be few. And we think it is very considerate of all you lovely ladies to consent to join us for this splendid dinner we've got planned."

It was clear that the two ensigns had visited several bars before they arrived in this one. We looked at one another for a moment, wondering whether we wanted to spend one of our last evenings in the states with two not entirely sober naval officers.

Alice seized the initiative. "It will be our great pleasure to have you two nice boys entertain us this evening. But we have a transportation problem. Our bus back to Camp Blanding leaves in forty-five minutes. If we stay with you, how do we get back? AWOL is not our style."

Paul was ready for this: "Let us not get bogged down in trivia. Our cadet friend here has a large, commodious sedan, and my roommate, Bill, has a nice sporty convertible complete with rumble seat and all that. Getting you ladies back to Blanding is not a problem." Bill had still not spoken a word, but he seconded what he heard from Paul with a sober nod of the head.

Florence (left) at Camp Blanding (1942).

Florence, Camp
Blanding (1942)

"Let's discuss this dinner we were talking about," Paul continued. "Do you ladies like spaghetti? All of you look so slim, I'm sure you could use some food that'll stick to your bones."

Alice liked that. "Flattery will get you everywhere. Sure we like spaghetti. Why do you ask?"

"Well, Bill and I know this place called Guipponi's. It's really an Italian grocery, but Mr. and Mrs. G. have a dining room in back with oilcloth tablecloths and a little sawdust on the floor. You know, short on decor, but the food and chianti are marvelous. What do you say?"

Alice didn't hesitate. "I say let's do it."

Guipponi's was as good as Paul had made it out to be. What he neglected to mention was that the spaghetti was sixty-five cents for a mountain of it in a huge bowl, and the chianti was seventy-five cents a bottle. So we didn't feel too badly that the two new ensigns were squandering their new-found riches on people they didn't even know. In any case, we felt it was the thought that counted, not how much it cost.

The cadet stayed with us for dinner, but he was so quiet that we hardly knew he was there amid all the boisterous talk around the table. I recall that his name was Scranton, and Paul remembers that he was related to the William Scranton who became governor of Pennsylvania and then our ambassador to the United Nations.

Cadet Scranton took three of our nurses back to Blanding while Alice and I rode with Bill and Paul. Paul and I were in the rumble seat, and we talked non-stop all the way back to camp. When we weren't talking, we were singing. I told Paul about my divorce just before I signed up for the Army Nurse Corps, and my hopes for seeing action once we reached Europe. He told me why he had chosen naval aviation and how much he wanted to join a squadron that would fly from one of the new large carriers operating in the Pacific. It was obvious that flying had become the most important thing in his life. Up front, Bill was not as animated as Paul, but he didn't have to be. Alice never stopped talking from the time we left Jacksonville until we passed through Blanding's main gate. All Bill got to do was nod every now and then.

I half expected Paul to make some kind of pass during the ride home. After all, it was wartime and the regular rules don't apply when there is such a great compression of time. Everything runs together, and there is never enough time during war to develop a relationship at a normal pace. But I was pleasantly surprised to find that underneath the outgoing and slightly inebriated manner, there was a rather shy, modest man. I knew intuitively he was so devoted to flying that everything else took a back seat, and that he was good at it. I could tell that from the quiet way he talked about flying and the way he moved and carried himself. He was much more interested in what I had to say than he was in telling me about himself. He didn't even try to hold my hand, let alone put his arm around me. I liked him for that. When we said good night at the entrance to nurses' quarters, he took my hand in a firm, warm grip and looked directly into my eyes. "Fitzie," he said, "I wish you weren't leaving so soon. I'd like to see a lot more of you."

As Bill drove off, Paul looked back only once and gave me a smart salute.

And then my world fell apart. The Army suddenly discovered that our unit had one more nurse than our table of organization allowed. We all put our names in a hat, and one of our doctors pulled out a slip. *It had my name on it.* I nearly fainted and began to cry at once. How could this happen to me, Florence Josephine

Fitzsimmons? I was a hard worker, a good nurse, I liked everybody, everybody liked me, so why me?

Over the next few days, I became a basket case. I couldn't stop crying, I couldn't hold food down, and I wasn't getting any sleep. The doctors decided to put me in the hospital, so they could sedate and monitor me. I was hospitalized for three or four days and felt a little better when I was released. But there was a heavy stone where my heart used to be, and I just couldn't accept that I wasn't going overseas. In the meantime, I was removed from the operating room and placed on night duty. I wasn't performing as I should, and the surgeons apparently thought I was too much of a risk. I'm sure they were right.

One of the doctors, a young captain, prescribed social therapy for my condition and asked me out to a football game in Jacksonville. I wasn't overly enthused, but I realized it was time I started thinking about something other than my bad luck, so I accepted.

During half-time, the captain and I moved under the grandstand with the crowd to find relief from a broiling sun. Standing next to me was Bill Green! He heard me out about why I was still at Blanding. I asked about Paul, and he told me Paul was training in seaplanes and doing a lot of night flying. He said he'd let Paul know I was at Blanding. I thanked him and we parted.

A few nights later, I was at my duty desk in the casualty ward, working on charts. I looked up to find Paul standing in front of my desk. He'd come in so silently that he startled me. He asked why I was still at Blanding and I gave him a tearful account. "Bill told me you were still here, Fitzie, so I called and they told me you were on night duty and where to find you."

"Yes, still here and no prospects for going overseas. I've got to get out of Blanding," I said. "Look, it's about eleven o'clock and that's my dinner time. There's a deck just out that door. Why don't we walk out there where we'll have a little more privacy?" By this time, half the patients in the ward, those who could, were sitting up in bed staring at the stranger in a white uniform. To be entirely honest, I was kind of hoping Paul would take me in his arms and comfort me. If that means I was a hussy, I guess I was.

"I see what you mean. Let's do it."

Paul on day he got his wings,
  Jacksonville (1942).

When we walked out to the deck, we found a carpet of stars and a slice of new moon in a cloudless sky. Paul looked up and said, "What a great night for night flying."

My heart sank. I thought, "What kind of clown is this? Here I am hoping there's some romance in him and he's talking night flying."

But I didn't want him to know I was disappointed. I knew how focused he was on flying to the exclusion of everything else, so I took that in stride as we talked about how the war was going. Finally, I had to go back in. Paul had driven fifty miles to see me for half an hour, but he understood. Before we went back in, he put his hands on my shoulders and said, "Fitzie, I want to see you while you're still here at Blanding. I'll be in touch." Then he bent down toward me. I offered my lips, but he chose to kiss me softly on the cheek.

A few days later, Paul called and said there was going to be a ball at the air station to celebrate a change of command. He would be honored if I would be his guest. It would be quite formal, he said, and the wives of the station officers were gearing up to make it a memorable occasion. I could come in my dress uniform, or civilian dress if I preferred.

For the first time since my name was pulled out of the hat and I was left behind, I felt a tingle of excitement. One of the last things I did before I crossed the line from civilian to soldier was to buy an outrageously expensive evening gown in New York. I had carried it with me through mosquito-ridden field exercises in North Carolina and training in rapid deployment of tents in the Florida Everglades. *Now by God I was going to wear it.* I didn't hesitate a moment in telling Paul I'd be delighted to be his guest.

I was not allowed to wear the gown without official permission. The head nurse at Blanding made a Solomon-like decision. She decreed that I must wear my uniform leaving and returning to the post, but I could wear my gown to the ball. I was delighted. I immediately called and made a reservation at a hotel in Jacksonville

Paul's naval aviator certificate, Jacksonville Naval Air Station (1942).

where I could change. Paul agreed to pick me up there. I was to meet him in the lobby, and that was fine with me.

There was a broad staircase leading down into the lobby from the mezzanine. I took the elevator down to the mezzanine, so that I could walk down the stairs and give Paul a nice little surprise. The gown was black velvet, tight fitting at the waist and hips, strapless, with a low-cut bodice meant to highlight the wearer's natural attributes.

Paul, dressed in crisp whites, cap under his arm, was waiting at the foot of the stairs. At first he paid no attention, as if I were someone he didn't know. But I was watching him closely. When he finally realized it was his date, I could see his jaw drop and his eyes light up.

"Fitzie, what a wonderful surprise! You're beautiful. Now I know you're of the female persuasion."

"I'm sure you knew that all along," I shot back. "You just didn't know *how* female."

The ball was a great success. It was a moving experience for me to mingle with these young officers, some of whom looked like they hadn't started to shave. In a few months, they would be flying from the carriers, testing their skills against the Japanese pilots. So, while I danced and laughed and joked with Paul and Bill and their friends, there was this doubt tugging at me about how many of these beautiful young men would survive the war. It was something to think about.

A few days later, the head nurse called me in to talk about my leaving Blanding. She said there was a large hospital under construction at Camp Van Dorn, not far from Natchez, Mississippi, where patients who were wounded at Guadalcanal and elsewhere in the Pacific were being transported. They needed doctors and nurses badly, and she was going to send a half dozen or so of us north to Van Dorn to help out. She said she knew Blanding held unhappy memories for me, and I was on her short list for transfer. I asked if this might accelerate my getting overseas, and she said she didn't know but it might be worth trying. I agreed.

I must admit that I didn't give Paul a thought in deciding to go to Van Dorn. He had, deliberately I thought, kept our relationship casual, and I had followed his lead. I knew he liked me, and I certainly enjoyed being with him, but it appeared to me that there wasn't anything deeper than that between us.

He asked me out to dinner at the officers' club the night before I left for Van Dorn. We kept the conversation light, but he gave me an address and telephone number where he could be reached, and I promised to do the same for him just as soon as I reached Van Dorn.

Van Dorn had been constructed during the Great Depression by the Civilian Conservation Corps, a group conceived of by President Roosevelt's brain trust to give young men jobs. The idea was probably a good one, but there was not a single permanent structure I can recall, and the place was a sea of red mud. I spent six months there. Paul called or wrote once a week or so, and that helped me through an otherwise unpleasant time. He came to visit once, flying a fighter plane into an airfield close by. We had a fine dinner and a pleasant evening in Natchez, but, as usual, the time was too short. It had been that way for us from the beginning. There was never enough time to relax and enjoy each other. We

Florence and friend at
Camp Van Dorn (1942)

spent our hours together checking the clock, always concerned about the time.

About six months into my tour at Van Dorn, there was a notice on the bulletin board about a hospital train unit that was forming up at Fort Benning, not far from Columbus, Georgia. When the unit completed training, it was scheduled to go to England. I volunteered at once and found myself on the way to Benning a few days later. When I arrived, I called Paul to give him the good news.

"Paul, I'm calling from Fort Benning. I'm here for training with a hospital train that will probably be sent to England. It was an opportunity to get out of the mud and overseas, so I jumped at it. What do you think?"

"I think that's great. Good for you, darling. Now tell me, how long do you think you'll be at Benning?"

"I would think at least three months."

"Good. What have you got planned for this weekend?"

"I know I'll be shopping in Columbus. I'm just about out of all the stuff we females need to keep you guys interested. Why do you ask?"

"Well, it just occurred to me that this would be a good time to drive up and see that you're being taken care of properly. That's one reason. Another is it happens that I love you and want to see you again real soon. And, oh yes, please try to find out how long the waiting period is for a couple intending to marry at Benning or in Columbus."

"Marry? Whatever for?"

"Well, you see, Fitzie, I love you very much and I want you for my wife, if you'll have me. I realize proposing on the phone isn't fair to you, but the Japanese made me do it this way." Paul's final comment was true to form. "So, if you've got nothing more important planned this weekend, let's get married."

I was thunderstruck, and it took a moment or two for me to get my breath back. I had no idea of how to reply. So there was a long pause. Finally, I managed to say, "Give me a day or two to think about it, and I'll call you back."

I tried to keep my tone as light as Paul's, but it was heavy

Florence at Camp
Van Dorn (1942).

going. I suddenly realized that Paul had probably had marriage in mind for some time. Now I had to make a decision that could make us both unhappy. My heart told me that I loved Paul, but my brain told me that if we jumped into marriage, we were bucking the odds. Our paths would certainly diverge, and then what would happen to our love?

Further, I had only recently extricated myself from a difficult marriage, and I couldn't see throwing myself blindly into Paul's arms. I knew Paul wasn't going to pay much attention to all the reasons why we *shouldn't* marry, so the responsibility for caution would have to come from me.

"That's fine, Fitzie, think about it. Try to think positive. Bill and I will be there Friday night. He wants to be my best man. I hope you can find him a date. One that doesn't talk non-stop."

"I'll try. I'll call tomorrow or the day after."

"Fine. See you."

"Yes, 'bye."

It was not an easy decision, and I spent a restless night. In the morning, I came to what I thought was a wise compromise and I called Paul. I asked that he and Bill come and we'd talk about it. Maybe we'd get married, maybe we wouldn't. Paul agreed to come, and we'd talk it through.

The next time I heard from Paul, he called from transient officers' quarters at Benning.

"Fitzie, we're in trouble. The sergeant who runs this place says he doesn't have any room for us."

"But the colonel in charge of our unit made the reservations for you and Bill for the weekend."

"Yeah, but the sergeant says he doesn't have—and I quote—'no rooms for two guys in Dugan Brothers uniforms.'"

I was amused when I finally figured out what happened. Paul and Bill had driven up from Jacksonville in their aviator greens, a work uniform. The sergeant was apparently from New York, and so was I. In New York, Dugan Brothers made bread—very good bread—and the delivery men on their horse-drawn wagons wore a dark green uniform.

My colonel spoke with the sergeant, and Paul and Bill had a place to drop their bags and come on to join us for dinner. It was a pleasant evening, but Paul and I had no opportunity to talk about our future. But Paul was particularly attentive and affectionate, and it was clear he was lobbying hard for a yes.

A couple of days earlier, I had discreetly inquired into the requirements for a couple to be married at the Fort. I found that Georgia required a five-day waiting period, so that a Wasserman—a test for syphilis—could be performed. I told Paul that while we were having dinner. I must admit I hoped that would eliminate the need for decision making because of "circumstances beyond our control."

But I hadn't reckoned with how enterprising a couple of ensigns could be.

"I'm sorry to hear that, darling," said Paul, "because that means we can't be married on the post. But Bill has checked on the requirements for Alabama. As you know, Phenix City, also known as 'Sin City,' is just across the Chattahoochee River. There's no waiting period there, all we need is a certificate of good health for you and me. Bill knows those are available in any drug store for five bucks a pop. So, if it will give you no great offense to be married in Sin City, Bill and I will check it all out early tomorrow morning, and maybe we can be married over there tomorrow afternoon."

I could feel myself being backed into a marriage I wasn't sure I wanted. But I loved Paul, I was sure he loved me, and I decided right then if he could arrange it, I'd do it.

Paul and Bill were in Phenix City by eight o'clock the following morning. Paul called at about ten and told me a story that became part of family lore. It seems that Bill and Paul canvassed a number of drug stores before they found one that could issue a certificate of good health. Here they found a short, round, bald man dressed in a shiny black alpaca jacket equipped with a pair of celluloid cuffs. The conversation went something like this:

"We're here for certificates of good health for a man and woman who want to be married this afternoon."

"Right," said the pharmacist, "I can do that for you. The certificates are five dollars each. But I need to do a physical examination first. Where's the young lady? I'll just take her back here to my examining room, and it'll take only a few minutes for the exam."

"Not on your life, Buster," said Bill. "Here's ten bucks. Take it or leave it."

The pharmacist took it. Now the boys had their certificates all properly filled out, to give to the minister who would perform the wedding. They walked the streets of Sin City until they found a Baptist church and minister who agreed to marry us that afternoon at three.

The ceremony was brief and the church was cold as a tomb. I wore my dress uniform and Bill and Paul wore their aviator greens. They had found several dozen roses and tulips somewhere in Sin City, and they made a valiant attempt to dress up the church. The minister had his hand out the moment we said "I do," but we were all too happy to be concerned about trifles.

My colonel gave us a fine dinner that evening in the officers' club. Paul and I danced until early morning. We spent the first night of our married life in Paul's room in transient officers' quarters. Bill took the mattress from his bed and laid it out in front of our door, sheets, pillows and all. He slept there all night to be sure we were not disturbed.

Paul and Bill drove back to Jacksonville the next day. Paul and I parted, not knowing when we might see each other again. It seemed to us we had been doing that since the day we met.

Perhaps a month later, as I recall, we were informed that the hospital train unit would be deactivated for reasons that were never explained. This left me high and dry once again. I immediately began to cast around for another group that might get me overseas. (I guess by this time just about everyone in the Army knew how determined I was to get overseas.) And this time I was lucky. I learned that the 32nd Field Hospital, then at Camp Rucker, Alabama, needed an operating room supervisor. I made a few telephone calls and was on my way a few days later. I called Paul to let him know what was happening, and assured him I'd keep him informed.

From then on, events moved faster than I'd anticipated. The 32nd was ready to ship out to North Africa in a week. We moved up to Fort Dix in New Jersey and Paul said he'd meet me there. Paul flew into Floyd Bennett Field on Long Island the day after we arrived at Fort Dix. The commander of base military police was kind enough to loan us his office for a couple of hours. It was as unsatisfactory a way to say goodbye to my husband as I could imagine. This time we parted really not knowing if we'd ever see each other again. But it was wartime, and we realized that our situation was not exactly unique.

3. North Africa, Italy

W E SAILED from New York harbor and disembarked from our troopship in Oran, Algeria, on the Mediterranean coast of North Africa. We were quickly loaded into buses and driven to the "staging area." Here we found everything from underwater demolition teams to the Massachusetts General Station Hospital, all thriving in an atmosphere of organized chaos. These diverse units were spread out over an area about two miles square, and there was a lot of training going on. Our corpsmen found an open space and set up our hospital and living tents. As soon as we were settled in, we began our standard drills for assembling and disassembling the hospital under combat conditions. A field hospital is normally sited about twelve miles behind the combat line, and sometimes comes under artillery fire without a

Florence, Italy (1943).

Florence in Italy (1943).

great deal of warning. The repetitive, boring training was aimed at moving our patients and equipment quickly and securely. We also did our share of marching in ranks and physical training.

We remained in the staging area for about two months, sleeping in tents and eating from mess kits. I somehow came down with dysentery, and spent a week in the hospital. Then we were told we were leaving for Italy by sea. My great adventure would become a reality! We knew our troops were fighting their way north in Italy, and meeting stubborn German and Italian resistance. Now we would be there, backing them up, caring for the G.I.s, tending their wounds and sending them back into battle.

The doctors told us we were to wear our class A uniforms on the journey over to the Italian coast. We never did find out why. It was something of a shock to our fantasies about going over to set up right behind the line. But an even more telling blow to our egos was the way we were unceremoniously dumped off a landing craft about one hundred yards short of the beach at Salerno. We were wet to the waist as we waded ashore. In our class A uniforms!

We set up our hospital in Battipaglia, about twenty-five miles south and east of Salerno. It consisted of about ten tents. When it rained, which was often, the mud was so thick and gluey that it took a lot of leg power to walk from my living tent to the operating tent. Eventually, the engineers came in and built duck walks and a few other conveniences for us. Battipaglia became our home base. As our troops moved forward—and sometimes back—a group of us moved with them. This brought me to Anzio, Caserte, Rome, Florence, Citavecchia, Livorno, Pisa and Verona. I lived in castles and beautiful old villas—and in the mud. We dined on pâté de foie gras and C rations—and we ate a lot of Spam. It was a roller coaster existence, very exciting, and I can't remember a moment of depression or unhappiness.

I sat at lunch one day in April 1944 and watched Mt. Vesuvius explode. The hot lava poured down the mountainside and, in a series of fiery explosions, wiped out two small villages on the slope. A blizzard of feathery gray ash descended upon us. In the surgical tent, we had to resterilize all the instruments. The ash was everywhere, in our tents, our beds and our food for weeks. It was a major catastrophe, and a sight I shall never forget.

We did what we could for the wounded every day. They were battered, dazed, bleeding and weak, and they were making sacrifices they never reckoned with. Many died on the operating table, and the loss of each of these young men—and America offered its best—was a personal loss for the doctors and nurses who labored to save him.

I have never forgotten a moment of my experience in Italy, and the work we did there. It was only a microcosm of what was happening elsewhere on several fronts, but it was our whole world, and we worked every day to save those boys, their arms, their legs, their strong, young bodies. So it wasn't easy, but that was why I came, and I was proud to be doing it.

Paul, meanwhile, had found his niche as I had found mine. He joined Air Group Two, made up of fighters, dive bombers and torpedo bombers on board the USS *Hornet*. He was flying a dive bomber called the "Helldiver." He wrote frequently, describing as best he could what it was like to fly from a carrier in wartime. He wrote that it was like a miniature circus on the deck before a launch, with the plane directors, gas "kings," ordnance loaders and plane captains in vari-colored T-shirts, all doing their jobs with practiced precision. As always, I could tell that he loved what he was doing, the danger, the excitement, the opportunity to use the skills he had so carefully acquired. But, try as I might, I could not bring together in my mind's eye a picture of what he was doing on a vast ocean so far away, risking his life every day.

Paul spent about eight months on the *Hornet*, and his air group came home to a warm welcome at dockside in San Francisco. He wrote and tried to tell me how proud he was of what they had done. He was also full of praise for his gunner, who sat in the rear seat, covered his back and helped navigate him home safely after each mission. We were to have a brief reunion with "Beano" Brigantino more than forty years after he and Paul parted. Seeing them together, even with both of them well past their prime, it was easy to see why they made a good team.

Paul came back to the States a few months before I did. While he was on board the *Hornet*, he had spoken with the air intelligence officer of his squadron. The AIO's family was friendly with

Paul on board the USS *Hornet* (1944).

Sumner Welles, than Undersecretary of State. Paul asked the AIO to arrange for him to be a one-time diplomatic courier to Italy for the State Department. State agreed, and the request got as far as the Director of Naval Intelligence. Paul called on the DNI when he reached Washington, but he was not able to persuade the admiral that this was something a naval aviator should be doing in the middle of a major war, regardless of where his wife was. It was just as well, I guess. If Paul had walked into my tent in Battipaglia unannounced—which is what he was planning—I would have had a heart attack.

Florence (right) in public relations,
San Francisco (1945).

4. Korea

AFTER MORE than two years in Italy, I received orders returning me to the States. I landed at Palm Beach, Florida, and was on the phone to Paul ten minutes after we touched down. He was then at Cecil Field, just outside Jacksonville, taking ten ensigns, brand new pilots, through a course called combat team training. Eventually, he would take the team to an air group on board a new carrier, the *Franklin Delano Roosevelt*.

We were very excited to be talking on the phone again, and it wasn't working out, because we were both talking at the same time. I was finally able to tell him that I would be at the Grove Park Inn in Asheville, North Carolina, for a week of rest and recreation. Paul said he'd apply for leave at once and meet me there. No ifs, ands and buts, he'd be there.

If saying goodbye to my husband at Fort Dix had not been exactly idyllic, our reunion at this magnificent old hotel was a truly memorable experience. It was autumn, and the leaves were just beginning to turn in the crisp mountain air. We were able to arrange for a room in the lodge that bordered the golf course, and we played every day. The food was marvelous, our accommodations were luxurious, and we spent a week filled with joy at being together again. We tried at first to pick up where we left off at Fort Dix but we soon realized that wasn't going to work. We had seen too much and done too much to try to be the same persons we were then.

So there were some awkward moments, most of them amusing. I can remember Paul asking me at breakfast one morning how I wanted my eggs. He was shocked to learn that I didn't like eggs. He said, "Good lord, I've been married to this woman for more than two years, and I don't know that she doesn't like eggs." You wouldn't expect a marriage like that to endure, but it did, it did for sure.

After Asheville, Paul returned to Cecil Field and took his ensigns to the *FDR*. I was ordered to Fort Lewis, near Olympia, Washington, to join a hospital train unit that was returning recovering wounded to their hometowns. I traveled from one coast to the other, with Paul meeting the train whenever he could. I have never been very good about time, and our all-too-brief encounters were marked by the pair of us running hard "like Bonnie and Clyde," trying to jump on the train as it left the station.

I left the hospital train for the Presidio, in San Francisco. I had been brought into the war bonds program, making appearances before community groups, trying to describe what the war was like, and encouraging our audiences to support the troops by buying war bonds. I enjoyed the opportunity for contact with the public. The people I talked with believed it was a just war, and they wanted to help, whether it was Rosie the Riveter or someone who could afford to buy a $10,000 war bond.

I was at the Presidio when the Japanese surrendered on the *Missouri*, August 14, 1945. Paul was training with the *FDR* air group in Chincoteague, Virginia. I had never heard of the place, and I couldn't find anyone who had. But I was able to reach him on the phone at the same time he was trying to call me. He asked me to apply for discharge as quickly as possible—I had more than the requisite number of points—and meet him in Washington, D.C. I agreed.

I was discharged in San Francisco. It was a moving experience for me; I had given a great deal to the service, and I felt the service had rewarded me in kind. I decided to take the Super Chief across the country to relax and catch up on my reading. I was lulled to sleep each night by the click-clack of the wheels of our pullman car passing smoothly over the rails. I slept late each morning, and never made it to the dining car for breakfast. I left the train in Chicago to do some shopping. My store of "civvies" was sadly depleted, and I wanted to find suits and everyday clothes for my new life. This was 1945, and I bought a couple of hats I was sure would make Paul forget the only hat I'd worn for four years—an overseas cap. This done, I got back on the train, and Paul met me in Union Station in Washington. By now we were reunion veterans, but there was something special about this one, a realization of permanence that brought us closer together.

We drove to Annapolis and took the ferry across Chesapeake Bay to the Eastern Shore, a long narrow peninsula that stretches from Delaware through Maryland and Virginia. It lies between Chesapeake Bay and the Atlantic. There are bridges now that link Annapolis to the Eastern Shore and Cape Charles to Norfolk, but in those days we had only ferries.

Paul had found a tiny old house in a small village, Onancock, about forty miles from the naval station. There was comfortable housing available on the base, but Paul chose to drive the eighty miles each day because he'd made good friends among the local residents, and he wanted me to get to know them. After I'd been there for a while, I understood why. Paul's friends ran the gamut from oyster fishermen to a U.S. senator—they were open, warm, hospitable and outspoken. They welcomed me warmly, holding back only a little, until I could prove I was as good as Paul had told them. I felt as if I'd moved back into the nineteenth century, living on this narrow, undeveloped, unspoiled enclave, isolated as it was from the mainland. It seemed to me that these folks made their judgments not on wealth or position as much as on integrity. Paul and I were still young, and we learned a lot from these good friends that served us well in future years.

After we had lived in Onancock for a few months, I became pregnant. Our friends were as happy as we were. Susan was born at a hospital in Nassawaddox, Virginia, in October 1946. She didn't learn to spell her birthplace until she was fifteen years old. We were delighted to have her, and the only unhappy note in her coming was the doctor's advice that I have no more children. But she was a joy indeed, as I walked her through the narrow streets in her stroller, sharing her ice cream cone with her Irish setter, with the locals stopping to touch and admire her.

When Susan was a little more than six months old, I decided I needed help with the housework and Susan's care. Looking after Susan's needs was a full-time job and left me no time for anything I might want to do outside the house. This happens to all young mothers, of course, but I believed it would be better for Susan and for me if I could find someone to help me care for her.

I placed an ad in the local paper and there were at least five applicants for the job, all of them from good, black, farm families living near Onancock. One of these was Mildred. She appeared for the interview in a clean, freshly ironed white blouse, dark skirt, and a dark blue wool watch cap resting on her ears. I invited her to remove the cap, but she politely refused, saying, "No thank you, ma'am."

Mildred had been raised on a farm not far from where we lived. She had attended elementary school out in the country, but when it came time for high school, the family told her she would have to find work instead. She said she was nineteen, but I thought seventeen or eighteen was more likely. She told me she didn't know much about housekeeping but was a good cook. I asked a few questions about her cooking, and then she asked me one I have never forgotten. She said, "Does yo' Birds Eye or does yo' peel?"

That did it for me. I hired Mildred on the spot and she proved to be a jewel. She was no great shakes at cleaning, but she was eager to learn everything and she was very responsive to suggestion. She had a native intelligence that served our purposes, hers and mine, better than any book learning. She was devoted to Susan, and Susan soon became a lot more interested in Mildred than she was in her mother.

I remember watching Mildred from my bedroom window as she hung Susan's diapers out to dry. She was humming a tune and tapping her foot, her body swaying to the music in her head, as she moved from clothespin to clothespin.

Neither Paul nor I ever saw Mildred without a hat. Nor did we ever find out why she wore it non-stop. When we had guests, she would dress up by wearing a red velvet beret in place of the wool cap. As Paul said, we never saw her "uncovered."

Paul enjoyed his work at the Naval Aviation Ordnance Test Station, where he worked while we lived in Onancock. He had transferred out of Air Group 75 on the *FDR* soon after the war was over. The station had almost every type of Navy airplane, and he could fly a different one every day. He was fascinated by the array of guided missiles tested there, most of which never got past the drawing board during the war. But it seemed to me that he was not entirely comfortable with what he was doing. And there was a decision to be made about Paul's remaining in the Navy. Before Paul joined the Navy in 1941, he had completed a pre-medical course and gotten his degree. He had expected to enter medical school the following year, but all of that was swept away by the war. Now he had to decide whether he should try to go on to medical school or pursue a career in the Navy. We talked about it for long hours; we finally decided that medical school at Paul's age would be hard on all of us. He had lost interest in medicine, he was doing well in the Navy, we were comfortable with our lifestyle, and we saw no reason to wrench ourselves out of it. Having made the decision to stay on, in 1947 Paul was accepted as a postgraduate student at the Naval Intelligence and Language School. He said he would never tire of flying, but he really wanted to exercise his brain a little, "lest it wither and fall out of my head." Neither of us had any idea what we were letting ourselves in for.

So we moved to a tiny apartment in Arlington, Virginia, and began a chaotic existence that is still vivid in my memory. Paul's classes began at 8 A.M. sharp and were over at 5 P.M. I had to take him to school and then pick him up promptly at 5:15 through rush hour traffic, so that he would have fifteen minutes for calisthenics before dinner. If I was ten or fifteen minutes late, it put a kink in the program, and I must admit I was frequently late. After dinner, he retired to the bedroom for three or four hours of study. There was an exam every Saturday morning from eight to eleven. On

Sunday, Paul would study in the morning and give himself the afternoon off. It was a nightmare.

It was probably the most miserable time of our entire married life. Even Susan wondered about her father's concentration on his studies, and how little time he had to spend with her. But when it was over, it was worth it. Paul finished at the top of his class in the Russian language. We had quite a victory celebration. All three of us went off to Vermont for a week, where we slept late, played golf, played games with Susan and ate our fill. What a wonderful relief it was to have all that behind us!

Paul asked for assignment to Moscow as assistant naval attaché, but there were no openings for a year. He was told there was a slot opening up in Sofia, Bulgaria, so he applied for that. For reasons never made clear, the Bulgarians refused to accept him. In this way, Paul was finally assigned as assistant naval attaché in Seoul, Korea, where the State Department was opening a new embassy.

The housing situation was uncertain, so Paul went first. I followed with Susan and Penny, our cocker spaniel. When I reached

Paul (center) at opening of embassy in Korea (1948).

Little Kim (left) and Big Kim.

Seoul, I found Paul had found us a very nice house and hired seven servants. Since he knew zero about running a household, I had reservations about seven in help. But the Korean domestics were specialists. If a girl did the laundry, she didn't clean or take care of Susan. For that there was a very special girl, Sunbosi. Once she met Sunbosi, Susan's feet hardly ever touched the ground. She rode around all day on Sunbosi's back.

From somewhere in the Korean Military Advisory Group (KMAG), Paul had found an old jeep for our transportation. He had it painted gray, so it would be recognized as a Navy jeep. We arrived at diplomatic receptions and formal dinners in our jeep, and this always raised a few eyebrows. We didn't mind that at all.

Our driver was a young Korean named Li. He spoke and understood English, but he had learned it from the G.I.s, so it was what we called "PX English." It was Li's greatest pleasure to brush up against bicyclists (he preferred old men) carrying saki crates piled high on the back of a rickety bicycle, and watch the whole mess topple into the middle of traffic. Whenever Li did this, it would drive Paul nearly out of his mind. He kept a riding crop under the back seat, and whenever Li was tempted to play the bicycle game, Paul would pull it out and rap him sharply across the shoulders with it.

Like most Koreans, Li was stubborn, and he never really gave up thinking about brushing Koreans off bicycles. One day he returned from taking Paul to work, breathless, red-faced and mopping his brow with the same khaki washcloth he used for washing the jeep.

"Anything wrong, Li? Are you alright?" I asked.

"Everything okay, missy. But big shit awful pissed off today."

Quite apart from Li, coping with the Korean servants made for an interesting challenge. Most of ours had been raised in good families, and they had been taught manners, Korean style. They knew what they had learned at home and they saw no reason why they shouldn't follow the same practices in our home. I tried to make compromises, but every now and then I had to put my foot down.

When we were getting started in our household, I gave instruction every morning to Big and Little Kim, the number one and two houseboys in how to set the table and serve food at family meals and dinner parties. Both Kims steadfastly insisted on serving Paul first and standing over him like a couple of vultures until they could snatch his plate away and serve him the next course before they paid attention to anyone else at the table—including me. I protested and Paul did too (but he was more amused than I was), but the Kims never wavered. Paul was the head of the household, he paid them, and he brought them their rice. It just didn't make sense to take care of others at the table before they took care of him. It was a painful conversion for them, but they came around to doing things my way when I explained that our household would lose face if our guests recognized that our servants had no manners. *That* they understood.

I had taught the Kims that a guest would signal that he or she was finished with a course by placing knife and fork together on the plate. One night Big Kim picked up all the plates on the table except the one that belonged to the wife of the French ambassador, who was the guest of honor. I caught Kim's eye and nodded toward the lady's plate. In white coat and dark trousers Kim stood straight as a Marine drill sergeant by the lady's side and said, much too loudly, sounding quite pleased with himself, "But Missy, she no put knife and fork together."

One night, dinner over, the Kims served coffee in the living room. The sugar and cream were passed, and I noted that no one, not a single person, took sugar. I drink my coffee black, but I made eye contact with Little Kim and signaled him over. When I looked in the sugar bowl, there was not a grain of sugar in it, and I suspected there never had been. I whispered, "Kim, where's the sugar?" Kim replied, much louder than necessary, "He don't know, Missy, none in kitchen." When I discussed the sugar business with him the next morning, Kim gave me a very involved answer for serving an empty sugar bowl, but, boiled down, he was saying that we would have lost face if the guests thought the household did not own a silver sugar bowl.

When Paul hired the servants, he was lucky enough to find an excellent cook. His name was Chang Li, but for reasons he never

Big Kim, Sunbosi, Little Kim and "Laundress Kim."

made clear, Paul called him Alfie. He was the finest cook I have ever known. He worked in the kitchen with a pair of long ivory chopsticks and virtually nothing else. Paul brought him into the dining room one night when we had guests, and we watched him carve a pair of wild ducks to perfection using only his chopsticks.

Chang Li and I got on very well. He was a short rotund man, built like Santa Claus and just as jolly, always smiling, always wanting to know what he could for you. When Paul and I took our dinner alone in the evening, I can remember Chang Li padding up the hallway in his felt slippers and peering around the doorway asking, "All okay, Missy, food okay?" It was better than okay, it was superb.

There was only one problem in this scenario. Chang Li was Chinese. The Koreans were ruled for centuries by the Chinese. The Chinese influence is clearly discernible in the fine, delicate touch the Koreans have in painting, sculpture and pottery, and in the respect and devotion the Koreans give to family. All that is fine, but the Koreans generally don't like Chinese, and they don't trust them.

This came home to us in our household when Big Kim came to me one day, very solemn-faced, and reported that Chang Li was stealing food. I knew that he had a wife and new baby living on the other side of Seoul, and that he spent his free day with them. I said nothing to Paul about this at first, but Kim came back to me several times, and finally I had no choice. Paul made small of Kim's complaint, saying, "What the hell, Fitzie, we've got more than we need, so what if he takes a little here and there? His wife and baby probably need the food."

"That's true, darling," I replied, "but the servants are upset. They think he's selling on the black market. I like Chang Li, he's the best cook we'll ever have. But we can't have this kind of discord in the house. Please do something about it, whatever you think best."

Paul liked Chang Li as much as I did, so he took his time looking into Kim's charge. Finally, he went to the embassy security officer and asked his advice. The security officer recommended that the police take Chang Li into custody as he left our house on his next day off and find out what he was carrying away. Paul agreed to that, but added that he'd heard how brutal the Seoul police could be, and he wanted to be sure Chang Li would not be mistreated. The security officer promised to instruct the police that there should be no rough stuff. So it was all arranged and we were both relieved.

Paul had a telephone call at his office from the security officer on Chang Li's next day off. "Well, Paul, the cops picked up your man today. I've got the arrest report right here on my desk."

"Okay, was he carrying anything?"

"Depends on what you mean by anything. The report says they searched him thoroughly, including a body search, and he had four prunes, a lump of butter the size of a walnut, and a few teaspoons of sugar, all in separate packets."

"Jesus Christ, where is he now?"

"In the local lockup. About a five-minute ride from here."

"Please stay right where you are. I'm coming by your office right now, and I'd appreciate your taking me to him so we can get him out of there right away."

"I'll be here."

The security officer spoke Korean and was well connected with the police, so Paul certainly needed his help. When Chang Li was brought from his cell, Paul's worst fears were realized. His shirt and pants were in shreds, and it seemed to Paul that there wasn't a spot on his body that wasn't covered with a bruise. Paul blew his top right there in front of the sergeant's desk. He shouted at the security officer and swore at the desk sergeant. When they finally got him down off the wall, he insisted that the sergeant apologize to Chang Li on behalf of the police force. The sergeant said, "I no apologize to goddamn Chinese." The security officer intervened and changed the sergeant's mind. Then Paul insisted that Chang Li be driven home in a police car. This caused another big row, but Paul was wild, and he finally prevailed.

Chang Li came home in style. When I saw his clothing and his black and blue face, one eye almost shut, I cried. Still crying, I rounded up the Kims and the rest of the servants and told them what had happened. Chang Li, smiling as always, stood with head bowed in front of the group. I suggested to Big Kim that he might want to apologize to Chang Li. Shamefaced and looking down at his shoelaces, Kim did, and we all went back to work. Thereafter, I put together a package of powdered milk, sugar and fruit each week for Chang Li to take to his family. I should have thought to do that earlier, so Chang Li would have been spared that terrible experience, and it was thoughtless of me that I didn't. He stayed with us until we left Korea, and he continued to serve us the finest food we've ever had.

Early in our tour in Seoul, we attended a reception at the British Legation. The minister was Sir Vyvyan Holt, one of the most interesting men I have ever met. He had been awarded the Victoria Cross, Britain's highest medal for valor. Most holders of the VC receive it posthumously, but Sir Vyvyan was one of the exceptions. He could easily have been a Colonel Blimp, but he was not. But he *was* eccentric. He was seen frequently striding through the city's narrow streets after dark in Harris tweed cape and deer-stalker hat. Tall, very thin, angular in build, he reminded me of Ichabod Crane. I came to admire and like him very much.

When the North Koreans invaded in June 1950, Sir Vyvyan refused to leave his legation, claiming it belonged to Britain. He and his two assistants, Sidney Faithful and George Blake, were taken by the North Koreans and eventually turned over to the Chinese. Blake became notorious as the MI-6 (Britain's CIA) officer who worked secretly for the KGB for many years. He was found out and sentenced to a long prison term. He subsequently escaped, apparently with KGB help, and then surfaced in Moscow, where he is living today.

Paul and an Army colonel who lived next door entered a Korean-wide tennis tournament as a doubles team. One of the teams they played against was Faithful and Blake. When Blake was discovered as a Soviet spy, Paul made light of the fact that he'd played tennis with him in Korea. Others did not, and guilt by association eventually became a serious matter. Absurd as it may seem, Paul is still frequently called upon to explain.

Paul was carried on the diplomatic list as one of the most junior persons in the American Embassy, which neither one of us cared much about. But Paul had a big advantage. The naval attaché office had the only American airplane in the country, and Paul was the pilot. He had flown it in from Tokyo, complete with co-pilot, mechanic and radio operator. Our ambassador was a bachelor, and he liked to travel. Paul flew him from one end of the country to the other, landing frequently on airstrips that had not been used for years, built by the Japanese in the twenties and thirties in preparation for the aggression that led to WWII.

The president of Korea at that time was Synghman Rhee. He had an airline which today competes successfully in the Far East market. But he didn't dare use it then because he could not be certain a Korean pilot would not take him to Pyongyang, the North Korean capital, where he most certainly did not want to go. Our ambassador took care of his problem by offering the naval attaché's aircraft. In this way, Paul flew President and Mrs. Rhee wherever they wanted to go in South Korea. Every now and then, when only one bodyguard went with the Rhees, Susan and I would fly to many places in the country we would never have otherwise seen.

President Rhee asked our ambassador if he could give Paul a ROK medal. Paul said all he wanted was a pair of ROK Air Force wings, and that's what President Rhee awarded him.

Quite apart from Paul's routine duties as assistant naval attaché and his piloting the airplane, I realized he was spending a lot of time trying to find out what the North Koreans—and in those days that meant the Soviets and Chinese—were up to. He began a pattern of work at night, and rarely appeared for dinner. I thought he might be talking with someone from the North, but he told me nothing except that he was "busy." I knew I'd get no more from him even if I pried.

He also started bringing home for late suppers a couple of colonels from KMAG, the Korean Military Advisory Group. I couldn't imagine why two colonels would suddenly find a Navy lieutenant attractive, but once again it was Paul's secret, and I left it alone. One day at bridge with some Army wives, I mentioned one of the colonels, and everyone sort of hemmed and hawed and looked at the ceiling. Finally, the wife of an officer high in KMAG said, "Florence, he's not just an Army officer. I'm quite sure he works for the CAI."

"What's that?" I asked.

"Some kind of super-secret national intelligence outfit. Fred calls them 'spooks.'"

"Yes, but what do the initials stand for?"

"Damned if I know. All I know is it's called the CAI."

I had read about the National Security Act of 1947 that created the CIA, but I thought it best not to belabor the subject. If someone like the colonel's wife, who was something of an insider, didn't have the initials right, that was a pretty good clue to how little was known about the CIA in 1949.

When I told Paul about the colonel's wife and the CAI, he took me out in the garden and grew serious. "You know, Fitzie, that's not something that should be discussed over bridge. South Korea is almost a war zone right now. We have no idea when the North Koreans will invade, but they'll come, we know that. In the meantime, the less said about the CAI or the CIA the better. Agreed?"

"Sure, but I did my homework and knew it was the CIA. Why don't you give me credit for that?"

"Okay, you're smarter than a lot of those ladies think you are. I've known that for a long time."

"Enough already, let's have dinner. I *know* I'm real good at that."

During the winter of 1949, Paul and his aircrewmen did a routine port study of Inchon Harbor. It's colder in Korea in the winter than anywhere else we've lived, and I remember Paul coming home at night half frozen. I also remember his telling me of his astonishment at finding a thirty-five-foot tide differential. If an American warship were to err in anchoring by as little as fifty yards, the captain could find himself high and dry in the mud when the tide ran out.

It was a fateful task that Paul had undertaken. He, of course, had no idea that Inchon would some day become a household name because it happened to be an important requirement in General MacArthur's planning, and that the American landing at Inchon would be portrayed by historians as one of the boldest strokes in military history. So it was pure chance that brought Paul and his aircrewmen to Inchon that winter to provide the information MacArthur needed for the landing at Inchon.

One day the ambassador called Paul in and asked, "Tell me what you know about a place called Chinhai."

"Not much," Paul replied. "I've heard the president has his summer home there. Why do you ask, sir?"

The ambassador never said much to anyone. I got on easily enough with him. We chatted when we met at cocktail parties or at dinner at his residence, and Paul would look on in amazement. He told me the ambassador frequently stared at him in stony silence, not speaking for as long as a minute at a time.

In this case, the ambassador was a little more forthcoming, but not much. He said, "I've had a request from the ROK chief of protocol. He wants to know whether we can fly the President and Mrs. Rhee down there in a few weeks."

"I've got a pre-WWII Japanese airfield guide that has information current to about 1939 on all the landing facilities the Japanese developed on the Korean peninsula," Paul said. "I'll look for something close by and let my boss know what I find. If he okays it and you want it done, I'll be pleased to take the president down there."

The ambassador gave no reply. He returned to the papers on his desk as Paul turned and left the room.

Paul went back to his office and dug out the Japanese manual. The descriptions were in Japanese, which Paul could not read, but he could make out the length and width of a grass airstrip right at Chinhai and the nature of the surrounding terrain. He took the manual to a Korean friend in the embassy for translation of the Japanese. He learned that the strip was about 2,800 feet long by 75 to 80 feet wide. That didn't leave much to spare, but it was safe enough if there were no terrain problems. There were at least two. Hanging over the north end of the strip was a mountain approximately 4,500 feet high. The south end of the strip and the west side were bounded by the sea. The prevailing wind was from the south. That meant they would have to slide down along the mountainside at a little over stalling speed and then land short enough so they didn't all wind up in the Yellow Sea at the far end of the strip.

Paul thought he'd better have a look. So he took the airplane down and flew low over the strip several times. The grass surface looked okay, but the strip looked short from the air and the mountain ominous. He didn't try to land. Instead, he flew down to Pusan with his co-pilot the following day and they took a bone-jarring jeep trip to Chinhai. They carefully measured the strip and found it was about 200 feet shorter than advertised. The seawall on the west side and south end was in good shape. There was a burned-out tower and small hangar on the east side of the strip. Paul realized if they blew a tire or had to swerve for any reason, they were going to be in serious trouble. The landing would have to be near perfect.

So they flew back up to Kimpo airport, just outside Seoul, where the airplane was kept, and measured off about 2,500 feet by 75 feet on one of the runways and staked out the distances. They got back in the aircraft and made ten or twelve touch-and-go landings, simulating the conditions at Chinhai. Here Paul's carrier experience helped a great deal.

He brought the airplane right up to the edge of the runway before he started his descent from about 4,800 feet. He tried to come down like a helicopter. When he touched down, he was more than 500 feet down the runway. But his speed was so slow that he was able to stop at about 2,000 feet. They would have a stronger wind at Chinhai, and that would make the landing even safer.

Having done all this, they took the plane down to Chinhai and made three landings and takeoffs there. They encountered no problems, and Paul was satisfied he would not be risking President Rhee's life on the Chinhai airstrip. He reported this to the naval attaché, and they went to see the ambassador together.

"The plane's ready for Chinhai, and I'm satisfied we can get the Rhees in there without great risk," Paul said.

The ambassador looked at him for a long time without speaking. "Good," he finally said, "I'm glad to hear that. I think the president's going down there for an important meeting. I want you to snoop around a bit and find out what's going on."

"Sure," Paul replied, "that's my business. Who's he meeting down there?"

"I can't tell you that."

The landing at Chinhai with the Rhees and two of the security team on board went smoothly. Soon after they landed, Paul learned from one of the security men that the president was to meet with Generalissimo Chiang Kai-Shek, the Chinese Nationalist leader.

Rhee's party knew that Chiang would arrive by air but they didn't know from where and they didn't know when. Chiang had given them a time span of three days, and would not—or could not—be any more precise. So the security detail set up an around-the-clock watch in the burned-out tower and everyone settled in to wait. About a dozen of Rhee's staff arrived, having made the overland jeep trip from Pusan. Paul got involved in an Oriental gambling game played with dice on a Monopoly-like board, and lost about $50. When he tried to persuade the Koreans to play backgammon with him so he could get some of his money back, they just laughed.

At mid-morning of the second day, the sentry ran up from the tower and shouted, "He's coming, he's coming. Two aircraft." Paul hurried down to the airstrip with the Koreans and noted that two C-46's painted in camouflage design were closing on the airstrip from the sea at about 5,000 feet altitude. The Chinese pilot made one circuit of the airstrip and then descended rapidly down the mountainside. He touched down about halfway down the airstrip going quite fast, and Paul crossed his fingers. The pilot hit the brakes hard and slid to a stop no more than twenty feet from the seawall at the far end of the strip. The second C-46 made a similar landing. Paul breathed a sigh of relief. But he couldn't escape a twinge of chagrin over the elaborate precautions he'd taken before landing at Chinhai. He knew Chiang's pilots were American-trained, but he couldn't imagine who had taught them to handle a C-46 like a stunt aircraft, particularly with such an important passenger on board.

Chiang and Rhee met for about four hours. The president had planned an elaborate dinner, but Chiang said he had to go. The takeoff of the two planes (the second plane was there to be cannibalized in case a spare part was needed) proved to be as bizarre as the landing. The Koreans, adhering to Japanese tradition, had donned tailcoats and striped trousers for Chiang's visit. When it came time for Chiang to leave, they all trooped down to the airstrip to wave goodbye. They were all over the strip as the Chinese pilot started his engines. Chiang was standing in the doorway, waving and smiling, as the pilot put on a burst of power to get his plane rolling. Chiang reeled back and disappeared, only to reappear moments later, supported in the arms of a burly security aide, smiling weakly and waving. The pilot blew prop wash all over the Koreans as he taxied for takeoff, and Paul began to pull and push them into a ditch at the side of the strip, urging them to kneel down, striped pants and all. They seemed bewildered by

Korean President Synghman Rhee. Paul is at right, behind Rhee (1949)

49

what was going on. At this point, Paul was convinced the Chinese pilot was prepared to run them down if they got in his way.

When he reached the far end of the strip, Chiang's pilot made no pretense of checking his magnetos or anything else. He simply wheeled around, applied full power, held his brakes for a moment and then let 'er rip. The C-46 accelerates slowly, and it just lumbered along for what seemed a long time. Paul crossed his fingers again. As the aircraft thundered by where Paul and the Koreans were crouching in the ditch, Paul could see the pilot moving back and forth in his seat, sweating it out, trying to will the plane into the air. For a moment, Paul thought he wasn't going to make it. But as he watched, the plane carrying the leader of the most populous nation in the world, the Generalissimo, a hero to much of the Western world, staggered into the air, dropping close enough to the water to throw up spray.

"Jesus Christ," Paul thought, "if that's the guy who flies Chiang around all the time, he doesn't have enough insurance. That's a goddamned disgrace."

When Paul returned from Chinhai, the ambassador asked whether he knew why Chiang had come to see President Rhee. Paul said he wasn't sure, but one of Rhee's staffers had told him it was because Chiang's troops were being slowly pushed off the mainland by Mao Tse-tung's army. Chiang wanted Rhee to know in the spring of 1949 that he wasn't sure how much longer he could hold out.

The ambassador stayed in character. He looked at Paul for a long time without speaking. Then he said, "That sounds reasonable. I'll report it just that way, so let's hope you're right."

As Chiang had feared, he was forced from the mainland to Taiwan and, in October 1949, Mao Tse-tung's Republic of China was proclaimed.

A few weeks later, the ambassador and Paul met in an embassy corridor. The ambassador asked Paul into his office and then buzzed for his secretary. She brought in a file, and the ambassador leafed through it slowly and brought out a single sheet of paper. Without saying a word, he handed it over to Paul. It was a letter of commendation to the Director of Naval Intelligence for Paul's reporting on Chiang's visit to Chinhai.

Paul handed it back to the ambassador, saying, "Thank you, Mr. Ambassador."

"You're welcome, Paul," was the reply.

That was that. Nothing more was ever said about the matter.

Paul knew the ambassador was an avid bird hunter. When a Korean friend told him that the island of Cheju-Do, off the southern tip of the Korean peninsula, was literally carpeted with pheasants, he decided to test the ambassador's interest in a quick hunting trip. Before doing that, he went back to his Japanese airfield manual and found that there was an open grass field—no runway or strip—on the island. As nearly as he could tell from the manual, no one had landed there for more than ten years.

The ambassador became uncharacteristically animated when he heard the news. "So the place is crawling with pheasant, eh? Sounds great. And there's a place to land the plane?"

"There are a couple of problems with the plane, sir, but I think they're manageable. There's a small grass field where it looks like we can land and take off. No one's landed there for years, so I'll fly down and have a look before we take you down. Then there's the problem of communication. There's no telephone on the island, but there's a weather station there. I'm sure the weather station has radio contact with weather at Kimpo. Once we get down there, I've got to know what the weather is like at Kimpo before we take off to come home. If Kimpo's socked in, we won't have enough fuel to fly all the way back to Japan."

The ambassador really didn't want to hear any bad news. So he said, "All of that sounds a bit dicey. But have a look at the field. If it checks out, find out how reliable the weather station personnel are. I wouldn't want to get stranded down there for days because we can't find out about the weather back here. And it looks like we'll have to spend the night on the island if we're going to get a day's hunting in. Would we sleep in the airplane, take a tent, what?"

"Well, my friend tells me there's a group of Columban Fathers,

Paul in Korea (1949).

Irish priests, who live there. It's kind of a retreat and rest home for them. I'm sure you're aware they're very active in missionary work in Korea. Apparently they've got a large place down there, and my friend thinks they'd be very pleased to put up the American ambassador. We could have Kimpo weather call the weather station on the island to let the priests know we're coming."

Paul had had earlier contact with the Columban Fathers when one of them in Seoul asked the embassy whether the naval attaché's plane could fly a priest out of a small village on the west coast to a hospital in Japan. Paul had been told it was the practice of the order to give priests assigned to Korea a few weeks of orientation at the headquarters in Dublin. The orientation did not include language training. This meant that a new priest would be set down in a remote Korean village and left to shift for himself, without being able to communicate with the locals except through an interpreter. This made for a stressful situation for a missionary. In some cases, a priest might resort to alcohol to help him cope. In others, the situation might lead to mental deterioration or breakdown.

In this case, Paul was told a priest had suffered a nervous breakdown and needed to be moved urgently to a Tokyo Army hospital for treatment. Paul agreed to take him if the order would consent to his being immobilized in his seat. Paul did not even want to think about an unstable, strong, young Irishman thrashing around in a small aircraft. The order agreed that the priest's arms and legs could be secured to his seat, and Paul took two of the most formidable Marine security guards from the embassy with him just in case the priest broke loose. All went well, and the priest was delivered to an Army doctor and several powerful looking corpsmen waiting at Haneda Airport.

Paul arranged for the weather people at Kimpo to call the weather station on Cheju-Do to inform the priests that the ambassador was coming down to hunt, and the ambassador, Paul and his co-pilot took off from Kimpo in heavy rain a few days later. The skies were clear over Cheju-Do and forecast to remain so for a few days. But the weather over Seoul would be uncertain, and the meteorologists at Kimpo could not say when the weather front would move away from Seoul.

Paul's check of the airfield on the island had revealed that the grass field was bounded on four sides by stone walls about four feet high. The field appeared level and free of large rocks. When they arrived over the airfield, however, there were a dozen or so cows grazing all over the field. Paul made several low passes over the field, hoping to frighten them away. They didn't move. Paul turned to the ambassador, seated right behind him, and said, "Sir, we can land now, but if we blow a tire or have to swerve suddenly, we're probably going to hit one of those cows."

The ambassador fixed Paul with a level stare and, staying in character, said only, "You're the pilot."

Fate intervened to give Paul a break. Just as he dropped flaps and wheels to turn into final approach, a priest with cassock skirt flying out behind him ran out on the field brandishing a long pole. He drove the cattle into one corner of the field, clearing a safe place for the plane to land.

The priests were delighted to have the ambassador, a Catholic himself, visiting them. That night they put on a fine dinner, cocktails before, wine with the pheasant, and cognac after. A young priest, the same one who had dealt so effectively with the cows on the airfield, was assigned to guide the hunting party to where the pheasants would be. The ambassador, Paul and his co-pilot turned in, convinced that tomorrow would be a fine day.

It almost was. They had no sooner left the compound than they started to see pheasants everywhere, in the air and on the ground. As they were walking, the young priest explained that he and his brother priests shot the birds for food, but also because there were more birds on the island than the island could support. So it was necessary to thin out the bird population as best they could, lest the birds starve. They welcomed the ambassador coming down to help them do this. The priest guided them to the center of the island, where most of the birds were to be found.

The ambassador shot the first bird. As soon as the bird fell, he and Paul realized they had a problem. The entire island was blocked out into small plots surrounded on four sides by four-foot-high stone walls. Flat rocks piled one upon the other had been used to build picturesque walls, but the stones were loose. This meant they had to jump or climb over the walls without dislodging the stones. The pheasants, as advertised, were plentiful. But they always seemed to fall on the other side of a stone wall. That meant getting over one stone wall to retrieve the bird and another to retrieve the next bird that fell. The young priest was as agile as a monkey. He was up and over the wall before the ambassador and Paul got started. By noon there were thirty birds in the sacks the young priest and co-pilot were carrying. They had shot their share of the birds, and were about even with the ambassador and Paul. But by now they were all so leg weary they never wanted to see another stone wall, pheasants notwithstanding.

After a light lunch, the young priest and Paul drove over to the tower where the weather station was housed. To his dismay, Paul found it was over two hundred steps up to where the weatherman sat with his radio. The young priest, still in his cassock, scampered up the stairs like a tri-athlete. Paul climbed wearily up to where the weatherman and the priest were already in lively conversation in Korean.

Paul, trying hard to catch his breath, paused for a moment before he said to the priest, "Please have him contact Kimpo weather and ask what the weather conditions are there now and what the forecast is for the next four hours or so."

The priest conveyed Paul's message, and the weatherman loosed a barrage of rapid-fire Korean that seemed to last forever. The response that came through the radio lasted even longer. Longest of all was the weatherman's report to the priest. Paul began to wonder what he'd gotten himself into.

"He says the weather is no good right now," the priest reported, "and Kimpo cannot forecast what it will be like in four hours. Sorry."

"Please have him ask Kimpo for the ceiling and visibility there now."

This prompted another interminable exchange. Finally, the priest said, "Kimpo says the weather is bad there now. They suggest you call back in two hours."

Paul had to know the ceiling and visibility at Kimpo before he took off. But he was hardly in a position to force the issue with the weatherman. He decided to go back to the plane and try to raise Kimpo on his own radio, but he could not get any response on the several channels he tried. He knew reception would improve greatly once he was airborne. But he felt it was only prudent to come back to the weather station in two hours. He wasn't sure his legs would carry him back up the tower, but he thought it was the best thing to do.

Paul talked it over with the ambassador and his co-pilot, and went back to the weather station as agreed. This time the young priest took his time on the stairs and Paul staggered most of the way. The routine was pretty much the same. A flood of Korean spoken at machine gun speed with very little result. Kimpo weather suggested they try in an hour—still no information on ceiling and visibility. Paul was frustrated.

The priest and Paul returned to the tower an hour later. This time they stood at the base of the tower and there was a lot of shouted Korean exchanged. Still no information from Kimpo on ceiling and visibility. That did it for Paul. He decided to take off and fly toward Fukuoka, Japan, where there were English speakers in the tower. From them, he'd get the latest weather at Kimpo. If it was bad, he'd land at Fukuoka and refuel. If it was good enough for a landing, he had enough fuel to get him back up to Kimpo.

The takeoff from Cheju-Do was without incident. Their thirty birds had been cleaned and neatly packaged by the priests, who knew how to take care of guests. If they had to spend the night at Fukuoka, the birds would not spoil. When Paul was within radio range, Fukuoka told him the ceiling was then 1,500 feet and the visibility three miles at Kimpo, and expected to improve. That was great news.

When they landed at Kimpo, I was there and so was the ambassador's limousine. The ambassador tried to give all the birds to Paul and his co-pilot, claiming they had done all the work and he'd had all the fun. They wouldn't hear of it, and a spirited negotiation ensued. Finally, they each took ten. Chiang Li was happy to fix pheasant for dinner the next night. The rest of the birds went into the freezer.

As Paul and I moved from the plane toward where our jeep was parked, it seemed to me he was walking very slowly. I asked, "What's wrong with your legs? Why are you walking funny?"

Paul shook his head and said, "You don't want to know."

About six months before the North Korean invasion, Paul and I were part of a group in the embassy that was given a "project."

This was to reconstitute a golf course on the outskirts of Seoul, one that had been turned into rice paddies by the Japanese during WWII.

The Japanese annexed Korea in 1910. They were not popular rulers. They were sometimes brutal, they forced the Japanese language on certain segments of Korean society, and they tried to convert by force an essentially agrarian economy into an industrial one. So the Koreans didn't like the Japanese any better than they liked the Chinese. They mourned the loss of their golf course to Japan's drive for aggression.

We raised enough money to pay for most of the materials needed, and we persuaded the Army engineers that working on our golf course was a noble effort. In something like four months, we had a nine-hole golf course. Someone suggested that we find the Korean who was the last president of the golf club and ask him to drive off the first ball as part of the grand opening ceremony.

We had a Biographics Officer in our embassy. Most of us knew him because he played a great jazz piano at parties. From Cab Calloway to "Home on the Range," he was always there tinkling away when the rest of us were folding and thinking of bed. He was also the CIA station chief. The only person in Seoul who knew that was our ambassador.

In any case, he did a thorough research job and found our man living in a suburb of Seoul. A few of us went to see him. It came as no surprise that his name was Kim. He was pleased to hear about the golf course, and agreed to drive off the first ball. Looking at him, we were far from certain that we were doing the right thing. He was short—even by Korean standards—bowlegged and skinny. He looked to be about seventy years old. But we were locked into the deal, and we didn't talk to each other about our reservations.

Paul alongside North Korean aircraft (1949).
At center is CDR Jack Seifert, Naval attaché, Seoul.

I don't remember how many media reps in Japan and Korea learned of our grand opening, but it became a major story, and they were there in force to report it. There were *Life* photographers and *Time* correspondents, people from the wire services and representatives from golf magazines in Japan and the U.S. We were surprised and a little concerned by the turnout.

Kim appeared on the first tee in the crested blue blazer he wore when he was president of the club, driver in hand. His wife was standing in the midst of our group. He removed the blazer, folded it carefully, and laid it on a bench at the rear of the tee. He checked his grip but did not attempt a practice swing. I had a frightening vision of a swing and a miss, and I had my fingers crossed hard for Kim. He stepped up to the ball and, with a fluid smooth swing, drove it straight as an arrow down the fairway for about 200 yards. A roar of approval rose from the crowd. Kim bowed modestly just once and walked off the tee. I turned to his wife to congratulate her and she said, tears in her eyes, "I knew he could do it. He's an old man now, but I knew he could do it."

When North Korean troops moved south over the thirty-eighth parallel on June 25, 1950, Paul was in Washington talking to the Navy Department about what he had found at Inchon Harbor. That meant Susan and I had to take care of ourselves. Li drove us to the embassy, where the mood was tense, but everything seemed under control. The naval attaché told me that the invaders were meeting little resistance and were advancing rapidly on Seoul. Susan and I, together with several other dependant wives and children, would be evacuated to Japan by air in General Douglas MacArthur's aircraft, which was scheduled to land at Kimpo within the hour. We would be allowed one suitcase for the two of us. If we agreed to hold Penny, our cocker spaniel, on our laps, she would be permitted to fly out with us.

I packed hurriedly, leaving behind most of our clothing and many cherished belongings that I miss to this day. With tears all around, Susan and I kissed each of the servants goodbye and left with them all the Korean won I had. Then we sped off to the airport. The plane was already there, engines idling, and we boarded immediately. General MacArthur's pilot, an Air Force major, knew Paul from occasional airport encounters, and he came back to where we were seated to tell us that the invading troops were already in Seoul's northern suburbs, and we would take off at once.

In Japan, we were taken to an immigration office, where I was told it would be necessary to place Penny in quarantine until we departed Japan for the States. I protested, and the major said he would take Penny home and care for her until we were settled in Japan. I was still trying to accommodate to what had happened to my family and myself in a few short hours, and I had to pull myself together to thank him for his kindness.

We were taken to an Army hotel outside Tokyo, where we stayed for three or four weeks. I encountered problems almost at once. Susan and I were on the same diplomatic passport, and we were *Navy* dependents. That made a problem for the sergeant in charge of billeting. He was not sure he had the authority to put us up in an *Army* billet. By now it was late at night, and I persuaded him to give us a room for the night; we'd settle the inter-service problem in the morning.

At breakfast the following morning, I was the only person in the dining room without a copy of the *Stars and Stripes*. The same sergeant told me he had a limited number of copies and they went only to Army personnel and their dependents (I never did get that one straightened out). When I asked for a PX card because I needed white polish for Susan's shoes, the sergeant said he couldn't issue one to *Navy* dependents with a diplomatic passport. There was a comedic aspect to what was happening to us, but I must admit I was not in a frame of mind to appreciate it. An Army colonel having his breakfast at an adjoining table overheard my conversation with the sergeant. When he learned Susan and I had just come from Korea, he gave me his *Stars and Stripes* and went off to the PX for my white shoe polish.

That was not the end of my problems as a Navy dependent adrift in an Army sea.

I scavenged copies of the *Stars and Stripes* from wastebaskets, lobby furniture, ladies rooms and dining room tables (the newspaper was our only source of information on what was happening in Korea), and I recruited a couple of Army wives to help me with my PX needs.

We stayed in Tokyo for three or four weeks until space became available on a Military Sea Transport Service (MSTS) troopship. Susan and I took several tours, venturing as far afield as Osaka and Kyoto, where I bought a string of pearls for myself and a pair of cuff links for Paul. Susan (she was then almost four) came off a weak third with a silver bracelet.

One day out of San Francisco, we were given a memorandum outlining the order of debarkation. First off the ship would be Army and Air Corps officers, then Army and Air Corps enlisted, then dependents of Army and Air Corps officers, then dependents of Army and Air Corps enlisted, then Susan and I. By this time I was so inured to what had happened to us since we left Korea, that I laughed when I read the memo. But Paul, down on the dock as the ship tied up, didn't think it was all that amusing. He watched the passengers pouring off the ship as Susan and I stood at the rail. He kept urging me to get in line. I could only shrug my shoulders and point to the memorandum I was clutching. When Susan and I finally got to him down on the dock, and explained why we'd been delayed, he laughed as I had. Then the three of us went out on the town and tried to eat all the cracked crab in San Francisco. It was one glorious reunion.

It was a bitter experience for me to leave so quickly and abandon my Koreans. It would not take long for the North Korean troops to learn they had worked for an American family. With no place to hide, they would be the first to be executed. I cried myself to sleep for weeks, knowing they had given their lives because they were so faithful to our family.

One of the first things I did after we were settled back in the States was to organize a Korean relief drive. We collected approximately 7,000 pounds of food, medicine and clothing. The Navy agreed to transport it to Japan. From there, it was taken to Korea and distributed to the needy by the Seventh Day Adventists, who were very active in missionary work in Korea. It was the least I could do.

•

Paul told us he'd been assigned as an aide to the Chief of the Bureau of Aeronautics. These were the McCarthy years, and the Navy was being bombarded with accusations of Communists in its ranks. There was little substance to any of the charges, but the admiral wanted someone on his staff who would respond to these letters quickly and politely. Paul did this for about six months, and I could see that he was getting bored and restless. The bureaucracy had never been a comfortable work environment for him.

5. The Beginning

AT ABOUT the time Paul was getting ready to try for another attaché job, he received a telephone call one night from one of the colonels he'd known in Korea, asking him out for a drink at a Georgetown bar. It was the CIA coming to call.

Paul took me for a long walk in the country the following weekend. He explained that the small cadre of former OSS officers who made up the nucleus of the new Central Intelligence Agency was painstakingly going through dossiers, looking for recruits. They were aware of Paul's record in language school and Korea, and the colonel had invited him in for an interview.

So Paul checked in at one of the old tempos that stood alongside the reflecting pool between the Lincoln and Washington monuments. At dinner that evening, he told me he had been greeted by a "porky fellow" who looked like a teddy bear and spoke beautiful Russian. Then he was taken through a labyrinth of dimly lighted corridors, where he recalled there were plates of partially eaten food in front of many of the office doors.

He was ushered into an office that was in total darkness except for a single goose-necked desk lamp. He could make out a "skinny guy" bent crab-like over an old portable typewriter. The introductions made, the pair then walked him through his life going all the way back to high school, all in semi-darkness. Paul thought his hosts might have been using some kind of new truth technique on him (i.e., his answers would be more truthful if spoken in the dark). Paul was amused by the contrived scene, but he grew serious when he told me what transpired after the interview phase. CIA was establishing a modest presence in Alaska (this was before statehood) and the mysterious pair wanted to know if Paul would be interested in becoming the first chief of station there. (Paul's rank was lieutenant commander then.) He would need about three months of training, and would then proceed directly to Alaska for a tour of about two years. Some flying would be required, and there would be frequent travel between Alaska and Washington. Paul replied that all this sounded like something he'd like to do, but he wanted to do it as a naval officer, not as a civilian employee of CIA. After a two-year tour with CIA, Paul thought he'd know better whether he wanted to sign on permanently. He was told that would be okay with CIA if Paul could arrange it with the Navy. Paul added that he couldn't commit to Alaska before he'd checked it out with his family. After he briefed me, I told him I thought Alaska would be a great adventure for all of us, and he called back and said yes right after he'd received the Navy's approval for the assignment.

Paul realized he'd lost a lot of ground in aviation by going to the Language School and taking a job in the attaché system. If he now took a tour with CIA, he would have no future at all in flying. So it was something to think about. He also realized our family life would change dramatically, and he didn't want to obligate me to that without my knowing precisely what was going on. I had lots of reservations about Paul's starting a new career with a mysterious group of people he knew little about, but I didn't want him to see that right away, because he was so enthusiastic about CIA and Alaska. So I gave him a big smile and a thumbs up, and he gave me a hug to seal the bargain. I figured we'd both know a lot more at the end of two years.

He began training in the Washington area a few days later. At first, he was home by six every evening; then he was gone until eight, and later until about eleven. He gave me no hint as to what he was doing, and I didn't pry. He did mention that he began his training in a classroom with an interesting mixed bag of students, all of them being very discreet about their backgrounds—even their true names.

Paul made it clear to me that he wasn't trying to play "I've got a secret" with me, it was simply that he didn't want to burden me with information I had no need to know. He said he was certain both of us would be more comfortable that way, and I did not disagree. This understanding set the tone for the twenty-seven years we spent in CIA. Paul told me what I had to know and kept the rest to himself.

When Paul finished the training, he telephoned the two officers who had recruited him to talk about travel arrangements and other details. The receptionist told him neither one could be reached through the number given him. In response to Paul's questions, the girl told him there had *never been* anyone of either name available at that number. Paul refused to believe he'd been deliberately deceived—why would they want to do that?—and he set out to find one or both of the elusive pair. The first thing he did was search out the office where he'd been interviewed, only to find a different person behind the desk in a sun-filled room.

After walking the corridors for a few days, hoping for a chance encounter with one or both of his friends, Paul went back to a trainer he'd gotten to know. He described the offer made him and what had happened since. The trainer thought about it for a couple of days and then introduced Paul to the chief of training. He made a few doubletalk telephone calls, and told Paul the Alaska slot had been filled while he was in training.

"That's a hell of a way to handle personnel," Paul commented.

"Yeah, I know, but we're still forming up and learning every day. We're not as good as Navy personnel yet, but we're getting there."

"So what do I do now, go back to the Navy?"

"Well, we'd like to keep you here if we can. I've got a few things going where we can use a pilot with your experience."

"I appreciate the offer, sir, but I didn't come over to CIA to fly. Tell me, where in all the world is CIA most active right now?"

The chief didn't hesitate a moment. "Berlin."

"Okay," Paul said, "that's where I'd like to go. What do you think of my chances to get there?"

"I'd say slim to none, because of the lack of cover for someone like yourself. But the chief of Berlin Base was here a couple of weeks ago. I know he's short-handed because he made a pass at two of my best instructors. Like I said, cover's going to be the problem."

Paul thought there was a way. One of his classmates at the Intelligence School was working in the Office of Naval Intelligence (ONI), and Paul thought he could count on his help. So he said, "If I'm able to arrange the cover, can you have me assigned to Berlin?"

"Well," the chief said, smiling at Paul's enthusiasm, "the assignment must be approved by the appropriate area division and the German Desk, but you'll have my support, you can count on that. And I believe your chances are good because of the way the Alaska assignment was screwed up. I wouldn't want the word to get around in the Navy that we're a bunch of clowns."

So we went off to Berlin, where things were happening. As it turned out, Paul's assignment there was a stroke of pure luck, for it became a springboard into the kind of things Paul wanted to do in the CIA. There were dark clouds later, bad ones, but it was all straight up for a while after Berlin.

6. Berlin

MY FIRST glimpse of the city came as we were making our approach to Tempelhof Airport, near the center of the city. We came barreling down the flight path between two lines of bombed-out apartment buildings, the very same scene we saw so frequently in the news during the Berlin Airlift of 1948–49. This was 1952, and the bombed-out apartments looked precisely the same, ugly scars on an urban landscape. I had only a quick glimpse of the rest of the city, but I could see that much of it was still in a shambles. As we wheeled left into Tempelhof, I looked east, straight down Stalinallee, pride of East Berlin. The front of the buildings looked to be in excellent condition but the back of the buildings, which could not be seen by pedestrians, were falling apart. The Russians had made a Potemkin village to impress Catherine the Great, and now they had made one in East Berlin to impress the world. I could also make out the Gedächtnis Kirche, the Kaiser Wilhelm Memorial Church, close to the center of West Berlin. I had read a lot about Berlin when Paul told me we would be living there, and I remembered there was speculation that the Berliners didn't want to rebuild the church because it represented evidence of indiscriminate Allied bombing during WWII.

Paul was waiting when Susan, Penny and I landed. He drove us through a long line of old and new neighborhoods to one called Lichterfelde West. There we stopped in front of a large, solid-looking house just across the street from the Botanical Garden. This was to be our home for the next two and one-half years. Paul had once again found the house and made the arrangements. Only this time he had restrained himself and hired only three servants. There was Pia, who was the cook and theoretically in charge of the household. This made for a problem, because she was such a gentle soul that she was incapable of ordering anyone to do anything. But, between us, we managed. Pia was living in Berlin when the Russians came. When she knew me better, she told me haltingly and reluctantly that she had been beaten and raped repeatedly by the invaders. The psychological scars were there to be seen. When she served Paul or any other male at the table, she remained a good two feet away. She would bend at the waist and reach out as far as her arm would allow to deliver the plate to the table. When Paul's male friends visited, she remained in the kitchen.

Then there was Sabina, who was responsible for the cleaning and making sure that Susan did what she was supposed to. The Germans are known to be happiest as disciplinarians, and Sabina saw to it that Susan bathed, brushed her teeth and dressed in accord with Sabina's strict regimen. The Korean that Susan learned in Seoul was very quickly replaced by the German that Sabina fired at her.

There was also a sixty-ish lady we called Frau Lehmann. Neither Paul nor I could figure out how she had attached herself to us. She helped Pia and Sabina now and then, and did some of the early-morning food shopping at the produce market. She lived in East Berlin, and Paul checked her out with the security people. She came up clean. When Paul was studying German, he needed Russian-German dictionaries, and Frau Lehmann could buy these in East Berlin for a pittance. We still have them in our library.

There was a large cherry tree that stood in our back yard, and what I remember about Frau Lehmann is that I came out back one day to find her at the very top of the tree with a canvas bag slung around her neck, gathering cherries. When I asked her to come down, she just laughed and went on with the cherries. We had them for lunch that day, and she came smiling to the table, wanting us to tell her how good they tasted, which we did. I finally figured out that she would respond to Paul's requests, but rarely to mine. I let it go. I didn't much like it, but I was busy elsewhere.

Soon after we settled in, Paul and I had a long walk in the Grünewald, while Paul explained our cover situation. He asked that I spend time socializing with the cover group. Only the chief of the cover office knew he was in Berlin for CIA, but Paul knew that over time many more in the office would realize he was "different." In the meantime, he thought we should both do our best to protect the cover.

This was not an unpleasant task. The ladies greeted me warmly, and gave me the benefit of their experience in getting on in Berlin. I played golf with them several times a week, we played bridge together, and Paul and I made it a point to bowl on their team. Eventually I had my own radio program on the Armed Forces Network station in Berlin, "At Home with Mrs. G." So it looked to me like we were doing what we could for the cover.

Paul reported that he was making some progress at work, but it was an entirely different world from anything he'd known before. Berlin Base, when Paul checked in, was lodged in a former SS

headquarters building in one of the better residential neighborhoods. Space was at a premium, and Paul was given a tiny desk in a room with four others, all of them living and working together about six feet from the entrance to the men's room. Soon Paul's clothes began to smell of the deodorant used in the urinals. I could tell when he arrived home long before I saw him. But Paul was enjoying himself, and he told me he liked the people he was working with. He described them as devoted and intense. He was trying to spend enough time in the cover office to

Florence in Berlin (1953).

68

"The Boys from Berlin." Paul is second from left (1952).

protect the legend, but, in his words, he definitely preferred the "men's room."

Following Paul's orientation, it came time to assign him to a specific case. When the Chief of Base learned that Paul couldn't speak German, he told him not to come back into his office until he could speak German well enough to do his business in the language. When Paul asked how he should do this, the chief, who was a legend in CIA, told him, "Any damned way you can."

So Paul went to the administrative and security officers and explained the problem. He was told he could study German only with someone who was security-cleared. He would do this in an assumed name with an overt reason for needing the language that would stand up to superficial scrutiny, just in case anyone got nosy. The admin officer said there were no cleared instructor candidates just then who spoke English. But there was an elderly German who had recently refugeed into West Berlin from East Germany who was bilingual in German and Russian. He was security-cleared.

Paul spent the next three months with this man. Five days a week he climbed six flights of stairs up to a cold-water flat in an apartment building that was half bombed-out. They sat there across a small table from each other, in their overcoats and gloves, for there was no heat and it was freezing. They walked around in parks a great deal, they visited the zoo, they went to the opera and movies together, all the while speaking only German or Russian.

Finally, Paul went back to the Chief of Base.

"I thought I told you not to come back in here until you could handle an agent in German. Do you remember that?"

"Sure, I remember."

"Then what the hell are you doing back here now?"

"I can handle an agent in German."

The chief called in a German speaker, Paul passed the test, and he was assigned an agent.

The agent was a fascinating man known as "Sasha." Paul described him as "a little China doll of a man," always immaculately dressed and obsessively clean. He was Russian by birth and had fought against the Germans early in WWII. In 1942, Russian General Andrey A. Vlasov surrendered his entire army to the Germans. Later, the Germans allowed Vlasov, who was strongly opposed to the system in the Soviet Union, to form a Russian Army of Liberation (ROA). Vlasov enlisted many Russian prisoners of war to fight against the Red Army. Sasha joined the ROA as an intelligence officer and was badly wounded parachuting into

Florence and Paul at masquerade party in Berlin (1953).

70

Germany. When the war was over, Sasha, as a displaced person, was held by the Americans in refugee camps until he went to work for the CIA Base in Munich. He had been working in Berlin for about two years when Paul first met him.

From Sasha, Paul learned that he was running "eleven whores and a one-armed piano player named Willi." The girls and Willi worked in a bar located near Karlshorst, headquarters of the Red Army and the KGB in East Germany. They were encouraged to pick up scraps of information about troop movements, the composition of units, troop morale, etc. They were also briefed to try to bring a Russian over to West Berlin to meet an "uncle" who was interested as an academician in what was happening in the Soviet Union. The uncle was a very persuasive Berlin Base contract agent who posed as a professor of Russian history. One of the girls actually brought her Russian lover to West Berlin and he agreed to correspond with the uncle after he returned to the USSR. Two or three letters were received before the correspondence died.

Sasha was responsive to guidance, well disciplined and easy to work with. But it was not all smooth sailing. Sasha drank. He was a lousy driver sober. When he was drinking and driving, he was a disaster. Paul described him as "the worst driver in the history of the automobile in Germany." Paul and Sasha could not drive around Berlin in Paul's American-licensed car, so they used Sasha's car frequently. Paul would not get into the car if Sasha had as much as a glass of beer. Not infrequently, Sasha was picked up by the Berlin police for driving under the influence, and it was Paul's lot to go down and get him out of jail (through a "cutout," of course).

When they first met, Paul tried to speak Russian with Sasha. He begged off, apologizing for having forgotten most of his Russian. Since this was obviously not true, Paul assumed that, for reasons of his own, Sasha did not wish to be Russian ever again— not in any way. So they sat around and spoke to each other in very basic German. Sasha's German was worse than Paul's and they had to resort to a Russian word or phrase now and then. Once, Sasha, with tears in his eyes, told Paul that one of his girls was sick. Paul assumed the illness was serious, perhaps fatal. Sasha used a couple

Florence and friend at
Berlin fashion show.

of words in German that Paul did not understand. When he
switched to Russian, Paul still did not understand. Paul consulted
a dictionary before the next meeting, and it turned out that the girl
had contracted gonorrhea.

Sasha was a man of many names—all of them aliases. In Berlin,
he was Franz Koischwitz. When he was transferred to Frankfurt
after we left Berlin, he became a Russian again as Igor Orlov. He
had many names and faces before Paul met him. If he remembered
who he *really* was, Sasha never told. Not even his wife.

The wives and families of the men who worked at Berlin Base
did not have an easy time. It seemed to me that there was a great
deal of operational activity, and most of the meetings could be held
only at night. So I might see Paul at breakfast, I almost never saw
him at lunch, and it was a rare occasion when Susan and I had
dinner with him. These conditions invited disaster for the glue
that holds families together, and caused a lot of grief for my
friends among the Base wives. But most of us circled the wagons
and made the best of a bad situation. We wanted our husbands to
be untroubled in their work, we tried not to make it obvious they
were giving their families short shrift—which they were—and it
was my judgment that the Berlin wives, as I knew them, did a fine
job of supporting their husbands and each other.

•

In June 1953, East Berlin workers staged a protest march that apparently frightened the government into asking urgently for Red Army support in putting down the "revolt." Within hours, Soviet tanks entered the city and began to roll through and over the crowds in the streets. The workers fought back with rocks and Molotov cocktails and were soon subdued. It was a horrible shock to us that the Russians believed they could crush people under their tank treads one day and sit with us in the United Nations the next. But worst of all was their brutal treatment of the East Berliners while the British, French and American military looked on helplessly, as did Berlin Base.

Paul, like so many others at the Base, soon came to admire the Chief of Base for his operational acumen and commitment to making a significant contribution from Berlin. Their paths crossed frequently after Berlin, and Paul's respect and affection for him grew. His wife and I became good friends, and we stay in touch to this day.

A few months before we were due to leave Berlin, the chief

Berlin fashion show. Florence is at far left (1954).

called Paul in and asked whether he would be interested in leaving the Navy to join CIA. Paul gave him the background on his assignment to CIA as a naval officer, and said he would be willing to discuss an offer. We had another long walk in the park to talk about how we were going to make yet another important decision in our lives. I knew it would be difficult, very difficult, for Paul to make a commitment that meant he would never fly from a carrier again. So he was wavering and so was I. I weighed in with a reminder that the Navy had been our home, a good home, for more than fifteen years, and I wasn't sure I wanted to leave home for the great unknown. We finally agreed that we'd see what CIA offered and then we'd decide if it was worth making the change.

Paul met with an official in Frankfurt and rejected CIA's first offer. There followed two hours of hard negotiation, capped by an offer of civilian grade Paul knew he couldn't refuse. When we arrived back in Washington, Paul resigned from the Navy and joined CIA. We were now full-fledged, honest-to-goodness "spooks."

7. Stockholm

SOON AFTER our return from Berlin, Paul was walking through a dimly lighted corridor in one of the old CIA buildings when he encountered the former deputy chief of Berlin Base. They sat down in a vacant office long enough for Paul to listen to an offer to send him to Stockholm as deputy chief of station. Paul explained that he wanted to stay in Soviet operations. If the job entailed only dealing with the Swedes, he didn't think he was the right man. He was assured he'd be given a good deal of latitude in running Soviet operations, and his concern about that should not be an obstacle to his accepting the job.

So, even before we had unpacked from Berlin, we were off to a new country, new sights, new sounds and a new nationality to deal with and get to know. Much as I had with Berlin, I looked forward to Sweden with a lot of enthusiasm.

Stockholm is built on a group of islands connected by about fifty bridges. It is called the "Venice of the North," and in terms of its terrain, it resembles Venice. But, unlike Venice, this a bustling, thriving city, the heart of Swedish commercial and cultural life. It is set among heavily wooded hills, and when I first saw it, I thought it had to be one of the most beautiful cities in the world. Exploring, I found contemporary, sometimes ultra modern, architecture living side by side with seventeenth-century buildings. And I found it squeaky clean, both the streets and the Swedes who pass through them.

The Social Democratic Party of Sweden came to power in 1932, and the ultimate welfare state was born. This form of government has survived by taxing its citizens so heavily that the incentive to work harder and earn more is the exception rather than the rule. Not long ago, a Swedish author known worldwide for her children's books was taxed at a rate of 110 percent of her income. This was not considered absurd in present-day Sweden,

Florence (left) at home in Stockholm (1956).

and she had to take the government to court before she was granted relief.

The Swedes have been as faithful to neutrality as to socialism, and this stance has served them well in terms of prosperity. Sweden's most recent participation in war was against Napoleon's troops in 1813. Throughout WWII, Stockholm was a major espionage center, with the Nazis and the Allies vying for sources and information. The Swedes observed the contest from the sidelines, frequently profiting from their willingness to provide the playing field for the competition.

The blend of socialism and neutrality is important because it is not possible to understand the Swedish psyche unless one accepts that these forces have shaped it. The Swedes, pleasant and hospitable, are essentially passive and cautious, much more cautious than Americans in their business and personal dealings. When we learned that we were going to Sweden, I went to the library and found a half-dozen books that we read before we arrived in Stockholm. We wanted to be ready for our new experience, and both of us found that what we read was essentially borne out by our individual experiences. The Swedes are indeed a pleasant, passive folk.

Paul knew the chief of station from headquarters. He was preparing for retirement, and he was unfortunately not well for most of our tour. This left Paul in charge with a free hand in operations. I remember Paul telling me during one of our walks in the woods—this time on cross country skis—that he was experimenting with a new technique in Soviet operations, and that he was feeling his way but it was going well.

Paul and I arrived in Stockholm together, so this was one of the few times he was not burdened with finding the house and everything that goes with it. We very quickly discovered that houses were at a premium and domestics were non-existent. While we were looking, we moved into the Grand Hotel, Saltsjöbaden, a marvelous old establishment in the Stockholm Archipelago. It meant a forty-five-minute commute to the embassy for Paul, but we were right on the sea, and Susan and I kept telling him the surroundings were worth it.

Hard work and perseverance paid off. We found a very comfortable house on two grassy acres alongside one of the fairways of a golf course. It was vacant, and we learned it was owned by a Swedish lady who lived on the French Riviera, and she wasn't interested in renting it. Through embassy contacts, we found someone who was a close friend, and she made multiple telephone calls to the Riviera to vouch for us. She eventually got a yes, and we moved in, delighted to be finished with living out of suitcases.

We knew we would be required to do quite a bit of entertaining, both official, and, more importantly, unofficial, and we would also need someone to stay with Susan, now ten years old, when we were out. I went back to my wonderful embassy lady, a Swede who kept the ambassador's social calendar. She told me I should be looking among the immigrants who came to Sweden to gain citizenship, a process that required a residence of at least seven years. There were Turks, Syrians, French, Italians, etc. She eventually produced an Italian named Gerardo, who had worked as cook and housekeeper for an Italian industrialist family in Milano. I interviewed him and liked him. So he came to live with us, prepared many of our meals, and was exquisitely attentive to Susan's needs. She fell in love with him. Gerardo was volatile, and he blew his top now and then, but he stayed with us until he was overcome by love and decided to marry.

Gerardo's successor was a middle-thirties German girl named Esther. She was single and had lived in Sweden two of the seven years required for citizenship. She spoke good English, and had just left a job working as housekeeper for an elderly bachelor. She seemed right for us, particularly for Susan, and I took her on for a month's trial period.

Esther stayed with us for a year, and then returned to Germany. She was a good cook and an impeccable housekeeper. She worked hard and never complained. Susan thought she'd been sent from heaven, and they chattered away at one another in German constantly. Esther's room was in the basement, and Susan spent most of her time down there, with Esther restyling her hair daily.

Paul didn't like her and she definitely didn't like him. Paul thought she was domineering and referred to her as the "Nazi." He thought she would have done a good job making lampshades out of human skin. Esther came from Gelsenkirchen, in northern Germany, right on the Dutch border. It had been obliterated by Allied bombing during WWII. When Esther learned that Paul had flown dive bombers, she somehow got it into her head that Paul was one of the savage beasts who had reduced her city to rubble. Paul didn't make an effort to point out to her how ridiculous this was, and there was always an uneasy truce between them.

When Esther left, I turned once again to the Swedish lady in the embassy. She came up with a Finn, Mary. My first impression of Mary was not good. She was at least six feet tall but so fat she looked shorter. She had only a little English, but I thought it was enough for us to get along. She seemed willing enough, and I hired her for a month's trial period, wondering if I was doing the right thing.

A few days after she started work, I came home to find Mary scrubbing the kitchen floor. She was doing a good job in a very unorthodox way. Her stomach did not permit her to kneel or bend over. So she was lying full length in the soap suds as she scrubbed away. I asked why she had removed the handle from the scrub brush, and she explained she did better without it. When I told some of my Swedish lady friends the story, they smiled knowingly, winked at each other and said, "There's a Finn for you."

One morning Mary was serving Paul breakfast. She came up to the table with a rabbit (a live one) under her arm, nibbling on some parsley that she had tucked into the neckline of her uniform. Deadpan, Paul asked, "Mary, what's the rabbit's name?" Smiling, Mary replied, "My rabbit name Oskar." I knew Mary was crazy about pets—she spent a lot of time playing with our poodle—but the rabbit was news to me. I explained that she could keep the rabbit but she could not bring it to the table. She said she understood and that solved that problem.

Paul joined the American Club of Stockholm soon after we arrived, and I joined the American Wives Club and the

Florence and Paul
in Stockholm (1957).

International Women's Club. We found that the Swedish business-
men and women were very interested in maintaining ties to the
Americans and, in fact, there were more Swedes in the American
Club than Americans. Our ambassador wanted representation
from the embassy in these groups, and he checked frequently with
embassy officers who had joined to see how things were going.

The year before we left Stockholm, I became president of the
American Wives Club. We raised money for many charities,
including help for the nearly 200,000 refugees who fled Hungary
after the 1956 uprising that was crushed by Soviet tanks. (I should
add that in each country in which we served, I found the embassy
wives interested in charity and eager to work to help the less fortunate.)

Paul's experience with the American Club followed a much
more erratic course. Shortly after he joined, about ten of the
Swedish and American members formed a group within the club
they called the "Joy Boys." The number quickly swelled to twenty-

five, and Paul was selected as the first president of the Joy Boys. Paul explained that this was no particular distinction, since it made him responsible for fixing the martinis that preceded the monthly luncheon. No dummy, Paul recruited a station officer as the assistant martini maker.

One day the ambassador told Paul he'd heard of his elevation to high office, and wondered whether a luncheon invitation could be arranged so that he could see for himself whether he should join the Joy Boys—if they'd have him, he added. I'd always known that Paul was a schemer, and here he saw an opportunity to get out from under the martinis. If the ambassador joined, the group would almost certainly want him for president, and Paul could hope the ambassador would want his own man on the martinis. So Paul said it would be an honor to have him as his guest, and the ambassador came to lunch with the Joy Boys.

When Paul and his assistant began with the martinis, the Joy Boys made it clear they wanted them very dry and very cold. Paul experimented with less and less vermouth. He began to get lots of compliments and it went to his head. In order to keep the praise coming, he swore his assistant to secrecy, and they began serving ice cold straight gin, not a drop of vermouth. The Joy Boys roared their approval at the next meeting, and Paul's ego ballooned.

Paul tending bar at embassy fundraiser in Stockholm.

The ambassador was greeted warmly when he came to luncheon. He had made a distinguished career in the Foreign Service, but he was still a shy man. So he tried to blend in with the group and not disrupt the proceedings. Paul noted that, like the rest of the Joy Boys, the ambassador had three or four of the "martinis" before the food was served. After lunch, he staggered for just a second when he rose from his chair. But he recovered beautifully and walked from the room ramrod straight and in full control. Paul saw him to his car; he tripped getting into the back seat and barely recovered enough to end up in a sitting position. Paul pretended not to notice and waved goodbye.

Paul never mentioned the Joy Boys again and neither did the ambassador. He and his wife visited us years later, and Paul confessed about the martinis. Always the gentleman, the ambassador had a good laugh and held out his glass, remarking that he already knew Paul made a "helluva good drink."

One thing that spelled certain disaster in Sweden was to drink and drive. There were roadblocks up day and night and *every* motorist coming through was checked. A lot depended upon how far over the maximum you were, but if you didn't pass and it was your first offense, the automatic sentence was at least thirty days in jail and suspension of your driver's license for one year. The second offense meant a jail term of up to six months and permanent revocation of your license. If you were foolish enough to try for three, the punishment was severe—up to five years in prison. (In retrospect, these sentences seem overly severe, but that's the way I remember them.) These were draconian measures but they worked. People simply don't drink and drive in Sweden. The Swedes like to drink as much as anyone. So, if a Swedish couple came to your home for dinner or a party, they agreed before they arrived on who would drink and who would not. I never knew them to stray from this "designated driver" agreement. The price was too high.

We gave a "Black Velvet" party one spring. Black Velvet is a deceptive drink, half Guinness stout and half champagne. It goes down like velvet, but it can bring on disastrous consequences when overdone.

One of our guests was a Swedish naval captain, a bachelor. I invited a lady for him who bore a remarkable resemblance to a well-known Hungarian-born film star. She came dressed in a beautiful, low-cut gown. The captain's eyes bugged out when he was introduced, and I noted that he drank a lot more than his share of the Black Velvet. When the party was over, he wisely chose to call a taxi to take him and his lady friend home.

He called the following morning to tell us he had a terrible hangover but he wanted to pick up his car, which was still parked in our driveway. Paul, also under the weather, said, "any time." So the captain came by in a taxi, stopped long enough to tell us he was off to a picnic in the country with his new girlfriend, and drove off happily to pick her up. He never made it to her apartment. He was stopped at a roadblock a few miles from our house and found to have more alcohol in his bloodstream than the law allowed. And it had been something like fifteen hours since his last drink!

I don't know how it was done, but he lost his license for no more than three months. But he was rather philosophical about it. He said, "Sure, I lost my license, but I found a girl. And she's a good driver—she takes me everywhere. That's a fair deal."

We left Sweden after more than three years there. I had enjoyed the rugged beauty of the country and the friendship of its inhabitants. Now it was time to go home and renew our acquaintance with our countrymen.

8. Moscow

WHEN WE returned to Washington in 1959, Paul took a couple of weeks off, and we looked for a house. We found one we liked and could afford in Virginia. It was convenient to the office and Susan's school, so it was a good fit. I busied myself with furniture and decorating while Paul worked at adjusting to a headquarters routine. It was obvious to me that he liked his job and felt he was making a contribution. I was certain of this because, now that we were home, Paul told me a little more about what he was doing than he had in Korea, Berlin or Stockholm.

He said he was chief of foreign intelligence in the Soviet Russia Division. He explained this was a staff position rather than a line job, but it gave him an overview of Soviet operations all over the world, something he'd known little about before. It also gave him an opportunity to contribute to policy making in Soviet operations. One of the first things he did in his new job, he said, was to suggest that the technique he'd used successfully in Stockholm be tried wherever feasible in CIA stations around the world.

After about a year in the SR Division, a group of senior officials of the Clandestine Service selected Paul to be the first chief of station in Moscow. He came home that evening so elated he looked like he was going to burst. He tried to play Mr. Cool, but he didn't fool me. As we had done so many times before, we had a walk around our neighborhood while Paul gave me the good news.

I was delighted for him, but my thoughts turned to the problem of Susan's schooling—she'd had difficulty in adjusting and her grades were not good—and dismantling a household I'd just finished putting together. But Paul made these problems seem unimportant alongside his enthusiasm. He promised he'd take care of Susan's schooling, and he kept telling me it would be a great pleasure for both of us to start all over again in a new house when we came home from Moscow.

After that, events moved so rapidly that I felt like I was on a fast-moving conveyer belt and couldn't jump off. Paul's solution to the schooling problem was to enroll Susan in a good school in Switzerland. Instruction would be given in French and German, and we felt Susan could cope with that. But she was only fourteen and had never been away from home before. So I worried. We wanted her to start the term with her schoolmates, and that meant September. Everything ran together for me, and there was barely time to get her to Neuchatel before school started. CIA friends in Paris and Geneva put her up and moved her along, and got her there on time.

Then it developed that Paul had to spend a month in London before going on to Moscow. There would be no housing available for us in Moscow for several months, so we debated whether I should wait in Virginia or in London. Paul asked that I go with him to London, and that ended the uncertainty. We moved into an apartment hotel called the White House—I liked that—and we walked all over London when Paul wasn't working. What we didn't know at the time but found out later was that our apartment was directly below the one the infamous KGB illegal, alias "Gordon Lonsdale," had occupied before his arrest.

One thorny problem was our poodle, Hansi. There is a six-month quarantine in the U.K. for dogs coming from the U.S., and we didn't want that. We found Hansi could *transit* the U.K., providing his feet did not touch the ground at Heathrow Airport. So I held him in my arms from Dulles to Heathrow. Then we had to get him on a plane to Geneva. From there, a CIA friend would deliver him to Susan in Neuchatel. It was a complicated operation, but it worked, with only one difficulty we hadn't anticipated. It was pouring down rain when we landed, and we had a tight connection to make for Hansi's plane to Geneva. Paul had to carry Hansi all the way across the airfield in heavy rain—feet never touching the ground—and we were both wet to the skin. That was a real mess. Susan kept Hansi at school until an apartment was available for us in Moscow. Then she brought him to us from Neuchatel. She told us he'd run away once to find us, and she was afraid he was going to try to run all the way back to Virginia.

At the end of November 1961, Paul finished his business in London, and left for Moscow. When he arrived, the Soviet housing authority made available a tiny room in the Leningradskaya Hotel, where no American embassy official had ever stayed. The room was so small he had to leave half his luggage in the hallway. Paul felt he was vulnerable to any kind of stunt the KGB might want to try. So he leaned hard on the administrative people in the embassy to get him moved to another hotel, but the Soviet "organs" gave ground slowly. It took him almost a month to be given permission to move into a small suite in the Ukrainskaya, an easy walk from the embassy. I will not recite here the litany of

Susan and Florence in Moscow (1962).

problems he had in finding three meals a day—many times no more than one—but it was a very bad time for him.

Susan and I spent Christmas in London with friends. It was a hollow celebration, since we were both concerned about Paul alone in Moscow, trying to get his feet on the ground. Paul spent his New Year holiday in his new-found luxury in the Ukrainskaya. On New Year's eve, he could see the lights of the Kremlin from his window, and he called me to tell me what it looked like and to ask me to come and share his "luxurious" suite as soon I could get myself organized. I was in Helsinki two nights later. We spent a marvelous day there exploring the city and shopping for food and other necessities Paul knew by now could not be found in Moscow. The top floor of our hotel had been set aside for sauna and massage, and we both had "the works," knowing what lay ahead might not be as pleasant.

We boarded the train for Moscow late in the afternoon. I tried to stay awake for my first glimpse of Russia, but the sauna had done me in. Paul woke me as we crossed the border. We came to a small railway station a few minutes later, and I got my first impression of what Khrushchev was trying to do about de-Stalinization of the country. A massive, white statue of Stalin had been toppled and lay smashed to bits on the station platform. No one had bothered to pick up the pieces. I drifted off to sleep in the comfortable berth with the thought in mind that maybe our tour in Moscow was going to be more interesting than we expected. It developed that I was right, but for the wrong reasons.

We spent about three months in the Ukrainskaya. We had a tiny living room and a large bedroom, so we were comfortable enough, even though the walls were lined with suitcases and trunks. But I became more aware every day that we were under almost constant observation. It began with the desk clerk in the lobby, who served no useful purpose because he did not have the keys to the rooms, and no one in his right mind would have asked him to deliver a message to a guest in the hotel. And there was always a knot of poorly dressed men and women in the lobby, smoking *papyrossi* and pretending to read newspapers. The next observation post was on the fourth floor, where the *dezhurnaya*, the "key lady," sat at the end of the corridor and glowered at us. Ours was shabbily dressed, sullen and discourteous. She surrendered the key grudgingly, and behaved as if we were her mortal enemies. I often wondered how long it took the KGB to train that woman to be so unpleasant. When I remarked to Paul during one of our walks to the embassy that the KGB seemed to be everywhere, he said, "It goes with the territory, Florence. We've just got to get used to it and not let it keep us from doing what we're here for."

Ever since high school, I wanted to learn to type. Realizing I would have no household responsibilities for a while, I bought a portable typewriter and a lesson book in London, and brought them with me. I would do the finger exercises and leave the paper in the machine, carefully noting where I had left off. When I returned, the paper was *never* where I had left it. When I mentioned to Paul that I would think the KGB could do better, he answered, "There are a couple of things you should understand. First, the KGB sees itself as the sword and shield of the Communist Party. They will go to astonishing lengths to protect Mother Russia and the Party. Second, these people who are following us around are not rocket scientists. They're mostly from the bottom of the barrel. That's how come there's no unemployment in this country."

We moved into our apartment in the north wing of the embassy in April 1962. It had been completely renovated and refurnished. It was spacious and comfortable, heaven after the Ukrainskaya. Standard issue for each apartment was a cook/maid who came from the Soviet "organs." We drew a middle-aged woman named Lyuba, and she was remarkably inept at cooking and household chores. During her time with us, I did all the cooking and practically had to show her which end of the broom belonged on the floor. It was obvious she was not there to help us. I recall leaving a photo of Paul and myself in desk drawer, never to be seen again—I thought. Months later, I was trying to coax Hansi out from under the bed, and there was the photo, standing upright between the lower part of the mattress and the headboard. There were several instances of personal items disappearing from somewhere in the apartment and turning up later in the bathroom or kitchen. If Lyuba had been instructed to snoop, that was okay. As Paul said, that went with the territory. But she annoyed and frustrated us because she didn't have sense enough to make even the pretense of putting things back where she'd found them. Paul christened her "Loob the Boob." I registered one objection after another with the Russians in our embassy who controlled the servants, and received in return only knowing smiles and the occasional wink. The Russians knew what was going on, and so did we, but we all seemed impotent against the power of the KGB. But I finally prevailed over Loob the Boob and her KGB controllers, and we were assigned a beautiful young Russian girl, Nina, who was eager to learn what she didn't know about housekeeping. As time went on, Nina confided in me that she was required to meet every week with "someone from the organs" and report on Paul and me. Nina was torn between her allegiance to me and the KGB. On one occasion, she took me into the bathroom, turned on the taps and flushed the toilet, and told me that she had sprinkled powder on Paul's shoes that would permit the KGB to track him wherever he went. Paul sent a shoe back to the CIA laboratory, and was told that there was such a substance on the shoe, and that Nina's information confirmed what CIA had heard from other sources.

But Nina couldn't cook. I was teaching English to the children of diplomats at the Anglo-American School, and I was involved with several wives' organizations, so we needed a cook to be sure there was food in the house when I couldn't be there to prepare it. Paul and I talked it over, and he remembered that one of the consulate officers had brought in a girl from Guyana, and that she was doing well. I talked with the girl, and she gave me the name of a Guyanese woman who might be interested in coming to work for us in Moscow. I wrote and eventually Kathleen came. She was no youngster, she was fifty-seven years old, but she was a treasure. Loyal, hardworking, dependable, Kathleen was one of the best things that happened to me in Moscow.

Winter and summer, she would take Hansi out every morning

to a small plot in the embassy courtyard set aside for the dogs. In the wintertime, she would put on at least four layers of clothing capped by a fur hat with earflaps we had purchased for her. When she walked by the shack where the Russian drivers waited, they had a good chuckle over this large, very black lady dressed as she was, with a prancing poodle at the end of a leash. God bless Kathleen, she was wonderful. When we left, we sent her on to relatives in London for treatment of cataracts she'd developed.

Nina was something else. I grew fond of her and she of me. After the shoe powder incident, I realized that she had a split allegiance, but that she had decided she wanted to be more loyal to me than to the KGB. That may have been somewhat naive of me, but all of my female intuition told me Nina was straight. Since she was the most attractive female local employee in the embassy, Paul thought she might have been sent to us for reasons other than housekeeping. He watched for that, but it never came. Nina behaved.

All of the apartments in the Moscow embassy were completely furnished, so the occupants brought only a few personal household effects with them. I was particularly attached to a floor lamp I had bought for our house in Chevy Chase, and I had it shipped soon after we moved into our apartment. Nina admired it, and I wanted to give it to her before we left.

She made it clear that it would not be good for her standing in the embassy or the KGB if she were seen carrying the lamp out of the embassy. It was not something she could conceal under her coat, so we devised a plan to transfer the lamp to her on a downtown street corner close to a metro entrance, where she would be waiting.

I recruited a pleasant young embassy driver, Afanasiy, for help with the transfer. I carried the lamp down into the courtyard at dusk. Afanasiy was waiting and drove me to the appointed corner. I climbed out of the car and deposited the lamp on the street corner as agreed. I got back into the car and we drove off at high speed. Out the back window I could see Nina dart out of her hiding place, grab the lamp and disappear into the metro entrance. It was a successful clandestine operation carried out in the heart of Moscow. Paul was proud of me when I told him about it.

I had made a half-hearted attempt to learn at least kitchen Korean, German and Swedish when we lived in those countries. But the Lord had not blessed me with the language aptitude He gave Paul, who, when he was active as a case officer, could conduct his business in Russian, German or Swedish. But when we reached Moscow, I was determined to learn Russian. I found some language primers in the Anglo-American School, and I found a Russian lady who agreed to be my tutor. I became so involved I dreamt about learning the language. At night, I would take my books into the bathroom so as not to disturb Paul's sleep. I didn't seem to be making any progress, but I struggled on. Finally, my kind Russian lady told me it just wasn't going to work. She admired all the work I'd done, but I was no linguist. So I happily put the books away, and began to sleep a lot better.

But I did manage to learn a few words in Russian that have stayed with me. We had a fine ambassador for our first year in Moscow, Llewellyn Thompson. He was liked, admired and respected by the people in his embassy. He was held in high esteem by his fellow ambassadors. Even Khrushchev liked him. His wife, Jane, was good enough to make available the ballroom in Spaso House, the ambassador's residence, for the embassy wives to learn something about ballet. Our instructor was "Misha," who had danced with the Bol'shoi troupe many years earlier. He spoke no English, at least that's what he told us. As he took us through the movements, he would sound out, *"Raz, dva, tri, chetire."* So I learned to count to four in Russian and I still remember how.

We had a stream of visitors during our time in Moscow, personal, official and some very unofficial. Two of our visitors were sent to us by friends retired in Florida. They were a married couple on a month-long visit to the Middle East, and they had come up the Black Sea to Odessa on a cruise ship. From there they flew up to Moscow and stayed with us for a few days. They wanted to give a party when they returned to the ship, and asked if I could get some premium caviar for them on the local market. The husband gave me a $100 bill, and I took this to the embassy cashier, who gave me 90 rubles for it. At that time, 1 ruble cost $1.11, a totally artificial rate of exchange, since the ruble has never had value outside the USSR. I think the ruble is worth about 6 cents today, and maybe even that's not a realistic exchange rate.

In any case, I took my ninety rubles to GUM, the government department store in Red Square. A very large Russian lady in a soiled white smock took my money and ladled out one kilo of beautiful caviar into a cone she had fashioned from yesterday's *Pravda*. That shook me up, and I hurried home to separate the caviar from the newsprint. Before I did that, I showed the cone to Paul.

"Florence," he said, "if it was our caviar, that would be the most *Pravda* I ever swallowed."

A few months after I arrived in Moscow, I began teaching English at the Anglo-American School to children of foreign diplomats stationed in Moscow. There were no facilities for food service at the school, so the children brought their lunches to school in lunch buckets, colorful metal boxes and briefcases. The standard fare was peanut butter and jelly, ham or cheese sandwiches, etc. That is not what the Iranian brother and sister I taught brought for their lunch. Their lunch was packed in an alligator leather attaché case and, more often than not, it was caviar. This was the gray Iranian Beluga caviar, the best there is, far superior to the Russian variety. There are few things I admire more than good caviar, and I must admit that I was frequently tempted to try to persuade the children to exchange a generous helping of the caviar for my ham and cheese on rye.

I visited several of the hospitals in Moscow, and saw the miserable conditions there for the doctors, nurses and patients. And I was taken to a couple of the *kolkhozi*, collective farms, outside Moscow, and saw the produce that never reached the market rotting in the fields. But it was my caviar-wrapped-in-newspaper lesson that drove the point home most forcefully for me that the

Russians were frozen in time, and this made every facet of their lives so much more primitive than most Westerners realize.

One winter Sunday morning, Paul and I were walking along Kutuzovskiy Prospekt, not far from the embassy. If Paul had an ulterior motive for our stroll in the slush, he had not enlightened me. We passed a bread store, and Paul said, "Let's go in and get a loaf of black bread. We haven't had any for a while."

We did most of our shopping in the well-stocked embassy commissary, but the black bread was better than anything we had, so we went in. The small store was jammed, and smelled strongly of damp clothing. Since we hadn't tried this before, it took us a few minutes to get oriented. We finally figured out that step one was to get to the showcase and point out to the salesgirl which bread we wanted. There was a fifteen-minute line for that. When we reached the showcase and made our selection, the girl gave us a ticket that showed the price of the bread. Step two was to get into another fifteen-minute line to get to the cash register. We paid there and moved into step three, which was to line up in a totally separate queue, where you gave the girl your receipt and she gave you your bread.

I couldn't believe it. We had struggled for almost an hour to buy a loaf of bread. The customers kept their heads down and waited patiently while the salespeople kept up a steady stream of shrill abuse, as if the customers were there to commit a crime. With this kind of gross inefficiency, is it any wonder there is economic chaos in the country today? What Paul and I witnessed that day was the legacy of a hidebound Communist bureaucracy that cared less for the Russian people than it did for the perpetuation of a system that was rotten to the core. I wanted to cry for the Russians in the bread shop that day.

Before we left Virginia for Moscow, Paul and I had a long walk in the Blue Ridge Mountains one Sunday. He explained that his assignment was an important one for CIA and the government. He would be breaking some new ground, and he would occasionally need my help "on the street." We would do a few practice runs in Washington to build my confidence.

He never became any more specific than that about what he was trying to do in Moscow. A few years after he retired, Paul gave me a book to read entitled *The Penkovskiy Papers*. It was written by Oleg Vladimirovich Penkovskiy, a Red Army colonel who had spied for the Americans. The Penkovskiy case has been described as the most important CIA espionage operation of the Cold War. According to what I read in the book, Penkovskiy was found out and taken into custody in October 1962. Shortly after his trial in May 1963, eight British and American diplomats were declared *personae non gratae*. I recalled that happening in our embassy, and I remember asking Paul about it. He was non-committal, and I assumed at the time he was not involved in any way. I did not put any of these happenings together until I read the book. After I finished the book, Paul told me that his station had been very much involved in the Penkovskiy operation.

In the fall of 1963, Paul had an experience that sobered him and left him with a residue of lingering regret. The regret has not left him to this day. An American couple from Indiana brought a packet of papers into the consulate. The husband was a librarian, and a guide had taken them on a tour of Moscow's libraries. His name was Cherepanov.

On the final day of the tour, Cherepanov gave the papers to the Americans and asked that they be delivered to the American Embassy. They did this, and the papers were taken from the consulate to Malcolm "Mac" Toon, then chief of the embassy's Political Section. Toon showed the papers to Deputy Chief of Mission Walter Stoessel, who was in charge of the embassy because Ambassador Foy Kohler was out of town. Without consulting Paul or anyone else, Stoessel and Toon decided to return the papers to the Ministry of Foreign Affairs. (There had been an incident in Warsaw a few weeks earlier, when someone on the street thrust a document into the hands of an American military attaché. The document was a drawing of "rocket sites" in Poland. Caught red-handed, the attaché was declared *persona non grata* and expelled. Toon and Stoessel concluded Cherepanov's papers represented the same kind of provocation.)

One of the first things Paul did after arriving in Moscow was to reach an understanding with Ambassador Llewellyn Thompson about "walk-ins." They agreed that Paul would be notified as quickly as possible—at the most within a few hours—of any "walk-in," be it a telephone call, person or document. He had the same arrangement with Ambassador Kohler. Yet Stoessel and Toon had not informed Paul for more than 24 hours. The Penkovskiy operation had begun with Colonel Penkovskiy accosting Westerners on the street, carrying a packet of dog-eared papers. Paul was keenly aware that the American Embassy in Moscow stood like a beacon of hope for those who wanted to join in the struggle to rid the Russians of the yoke of a tyrannical ruling class. Penkovskiy II was always a possibility.

He was invited into the secure room, where he was shown the package and told without preamble that it was to be returned to the Ministry of Foreign Affairs in about an hour. Paul voiced his displeasure at being notified so late, and not having been part of the decision-making with regard to the papers. He asked that he be allowed to review the papers, and Stoessel and Toon reluctantly agreed.

The documents appeared to have originated in the Second Chief Directorate of the KGB, responsible for monitoring the activities of foreigners in Moscow and mounting operations against them. There was information about the drinking and sex habits of American Embassy personnel (i.e., who might be a promising target for a sexual-entrapment [heterosexual or homosexual] operation, who was thought to be an alcoholic, etc.). This did not look like provocation material. It seemed much more likely it came from someone trying to establish his authenticity as an officer of the Second Chief Directorate.

After scanning the material, Paul took it around to the Army Attaché's office, where they had a photocopy device. There were no Xerox machines in the secure area of the embassy, and copies could be made only by hand photography. He made the copies himself and secured them in his safe.

Then he went back to Stoessel's office and asked for another meeting in the secure room with Stoessel and Toon.

"Walter," Paul said, "if you return these papers, you're making a terrible mistake. It's my best judgment this stuff comes right out of KGB files. This is the kind of material that would come from a KGBnik who wants to talk to us, not what the KGB would use to provoke us. If they wanted to do that, they'd send us documents about military hardware, nuclear weapons, rocket sites, that kind of thing.

"But what is most important here is that there is no way they can provoke us with this material. It walked in here, we didn't go out and get it from a Soviet source. *You have absolutely no responsibility to return it.* You don't think the KGB's going to come in here and search our files until they find it and then throw us all out for espionage? What you're doing just doesn't make any sense.

"Lastly, if you return it, it will take the KGB less than an hour to trace out who gave the material to those folks from Indiana. Cherepanov would be up against the wall tomorrow morning."

"Well, you guys in CIA kill people every day," Toon said, "so what difference does it make if you kill one more? It's too late anyway, the stuff's on the way to the ministry right now."

Paul gave a millisecond's thought to inflicting some kind of mayhem on Toon right there in the secure room, but there wasn't time for that. He checked his watch. "But you told me twelve noon. It's ten minutes to twelve. Who's taking the papers back, Walter?"

"Tom Fain," Stoessel replied.

Paul left the secure room and went to the nearest window that looked out on the courtyard. There was Fain, the consul, standing by one of the embassy Fords, apparently waiting for a driver.

Paul ran down nine flights of stairs and out into the courtyard. He grabbed the envelope from Fain with a quick, "Sorry, Tom."

Back up in Stoessel's office, Paul said, "Walter, I'll risk my life and reputation on this. Don't give these papers back. A man's life is at stake."

Stoessel started to ring for Toon. Paul interrupted him. "I don't want to talk to Mac, I want to talk to *you.*"

Walter Stoessel was a mild-mannered, thoughtful man. He worked hard and had a well-deserved reputation for honesty. We occupied the apartment just above where he lived with his wife, Mary Ann. We liked them both, and it appeared they felt the same way about us. Now Walter was adamant about giving the papers back, and Paul has never been able to understand why. A possible explanation was that Walter was also a cautious man, and it was possible with Ambassador Kohler away from his post, Walter felt that there was less risk of a mistake if he gave the papers back than if he kept them.

Paul thought for a while about simply locking the papers in his safe and telling Stoessel and Toon they belonged to the CIA, but he knew there would be hell to pay all the way back to Washington, and that might be the end of a CIA station in Moscow. So he just shook his head and said, "Walter, you're wrong as hell on this one." Then he went back down to the courtyard (this time he used the elevator) and returned the package to Tom Fain, who looked at him like he was a lunatic.

Ambassador Kohler returned to Moscow a week or so later. Paul asked to meet with him and Stoessel and Toon in the secure room. There he expressed his deep concern about the cavalier way in which Cherepanov's life had been risked and the loss of a potential asset of great importance to the United States. He also stressed his regret that it had taken so long to inform him of the Cherepanov papers, and made it clear that he wanted to know about such things immediately at any time of day or night. Ambassador Kohler was an able diplomat; he didn't say so, but he certainly left Paul with the impression that there would not be a repetition of the Cherepanov scenario.

A few years later, a KGB defector evaluated as genuine told his CIA interviewers that Cherepanov learned that the KGB was on to him and fled Moscow. He was apprehended near the Turkish border and brought back to Moscow. The same defector said that he heard Cherepanov was thrown into a blazing furnace before a group of KGB trainees to emphasize graphically that treason against Mother Russia could be costly.

Walter Stoessel became our ambassador to the USSR in 1974. He died in 1986. Mac Toon succeeded him in Moscow and served as ambassador from 1976 to 1979. Looking back on the Cherepanov incident, Paul said, "Florence, there's got to be something wrong with my judgment, arguing with those fellows as I did. They go on to become ambassadors, and I go on to become one of CIA's prime suspects as a KGB mole. That doesn't say much for my smarts."

One Sunday morning, Paul suggested we go for a long walk. It was a fine spring day, and it sounded like a good idea. As soon as we were out on the street, Paul told me were going to Gorkiy Park. He had been waiting for good weather on a Sunday. We would behave like a couple of Americans from the embassy taking in the sights. He was certain we would be followed to the park and would be under close observation after we got there. He had something to do, he said, that required us to stroll in the park for a while and then sit on a bench briefly. If the bench was occupied, we'd wait until it was vacant. I was to sit to the right of him, so as to screen from view what he was doing with his right hand. His final words were, "There's no risk, Florence, so don't worry about it." I wasn't so sure.

The park was teeming with Russians enjoying their day off in the sunshine, and we fell in with them as naturally as we could. We walked along the river bank for a while, checking out the boats tied up there, just kind of rubbernecking. Then we moved into the park and walked aimlessly for a while. Then I felt the pressure of Paul's hand on my elbow, directing me toward a bench that stood against an embankment. Paul said, "It's been a long walk. Would you like to rest for a moment? Then we can go back to the embassy and have lunch. That okay?"

I nodded agreement, and we sat down. We rested there for a moment; then I felt Paul's hand moving toward the back of the bench. He fished around back there for a while, and then I heard him grunt, and his hand moved into his raincoat pocket. A few minutes later, we left the bench and started back to the embassy.

"Now, that wasn't so bad, was it"? Paul asked.

"Nope," I replied, "but I don't want to play that game every day."

•

Every now and then I was able to drag Paul out to the "commission shops." These were government stores that sold articles left by owners who could no longer afford to keep them. The owners paid the stores a percentage of whatever their property sold for. Some of the things I bought in those shops I could not have found anywhere else outside a museum.

One weekend, Paul surprised me by asking whether I'd like to visit some of the shops. There are few things he dislikes more than shopping, so I jumped on his offer before he could change his mind. We walked from the embassy down to one of Moscow's best shopping streets—not Rodeo Drive exactly, but very good for Moscow.

On the way, Paul explained, "I've got something to do that's very simple. I want you to get between me and the surveillants, so they won't see what I'm doing. It's the same stuff we practiced in Washington. Just follow my lead, and we'll be back in the embassy before you know it."

We browsed through a couple of shops, and I bought a pair of crystal candlesticks that came from an Old Believers church in Zagorsk, a monastery village not far from Moscow. I have them on my sideboard now.

I started to give the package to Paul to carry, but he said, "No, you carry it."

I assumed he wanted both hands free for whatever he wanted to do. As we walked up the street, he nudged me gently toward the entrance to a movie theater. It was barely noon, and the ticket window was closed and the entrance deserted. Paul stopped in front of a tall billboard that displayed the coming attractions in one column and the dates in another. He kept his back to the street as if he was scanning the board and so did I. Then he turned and left one hand behind his back. As he did this, I moved to screen him more completely and stepped on his feet and bumped him. He looked at me in astonishment and then grinned. I didn't grin back, I was horrified. But when I peered around him, I could see a black mark next to one of the dates. I never saw Paul make the mark, so I was relieved.

"Florence," he said later, "it's a good thing the two guys tailing us decided to wait down the street, otherwise they would have had a good laugh watching us behave like Laurel and Hardy. The trouble with you is the Lord didn't make you sneaky, like He did me."

One of Paul's cover duties in Moscow was frequent in-country travel. Sometimes he traveled with someone from the cover office, other times it was with an officer from another embassy. In this way, he traversed the vast country from Murmansk in the north to Batumi in the south, and from Leningrad in the west to Irkutsk in the east.

They traveled mostly by air. This meant a seat over the wing or close to one of the engines. In either case, it was always a seat with restricted visibility out of the aircraft. The aircraft then in service with Aeroflot was the TU-101, the first jet passenger plane in commercial service. Paul described it as a "dog," a dangerous one. One of the inside seats on the TU-101 had no window next to it. One of his fellow travelers, no matter what, was always assigned to that seat. He was always ready. He carried a small American flag and a roll of scotch tape. Much to the dismay of the flight atten-

Paul in Leningrad (1962).

dants, he would tape the flag up over where the window should have been and promptly fall asleep.

Paul and a companion from the cover office traveled to Alma Ata in Kazakhstan in mid-winter 1963. They were walking in a suburb of the city, followed by a surveillance Volga disguised as a taxicab, when Paul's companion (I will call him Sam) fell through a sheet of ice covering the sidewalk. Paul was walking in the road and heard a loud snap as Sam went through the ice. He hurried over to where Sam lay to hear him say, "Damn, I think I broke my leg."

They raised Sam's trouser leg as far as they could and saw an ugly bruise about midway up the shin bone. There was no bone protruding through the skin, but there was a definite bend in the bone where it should have been straight. Sam was in considerable pain and they were miles from their hotel, so Paul looked up and hailed the "taxicab" behind them. As if propelled by giant springs, the man in the passenger seat and the two men in the rear seat shot out of the Volga. At the same time, the driver took off his fur *shapka* and put on the billed cap worn by many cab drivers. Then he drove quickly over to where Sam lay, climbed out of the "taxi," and helped Paul load Sam into the back seat. Then he asked, "Where to?"

"To the nearest hospital," Paul replied.

"No hospital," said Sam from behind them. "Let's go back to the hotel."

"Sam, your leg is broken. We've got to have a doctor set the bone. Much better now than later."

"I don't want a Russian doctor messing with my leg. No Russian doctor."

"Sam, if we're lucky and the KGB lets us change our travel plans, we're still more than eight hours away from Moscow and our doctor in the embassy. And I remember that we can't fly direct, we're going to have to change planes in Tbilisi. You can't do that on a broken leg that hasn't been set. I want a doctor at the hospital to take care of you and maybe keep you overnight to be sure you're okay to travel. I'll stay in the hospital with you if you like. And we'll get something for the pain."

"No Russian doctor, no Russian hospital, no Russian pain killer." Sam was adamant.

"Okay, it's your leg, but I think it's foolish not to have it cared for right away. I've got a bottle of aspirin in my toilet kit, you're welcome to that. I'll see what I can do about getting a flight out of here to Tbilisi and then another back to Moscow. If we're lucky and the KGB cooperates, we can be back in Moscow by midnight."

The driver tried to make it look like he wasn't interested in the conversation. But Paul had asked in Russian to be taken to the hospital, and now they had arrived at the hotel. This was no dumb surveillant. So all of the conversation would be conveyed to the KGB, and that was fine with Paul. He and Sam were going to need all the help they could get.

He and the driver half carried, half dragged Sam into the lobby and up to their room. Paul paid off the driver and gave him a generous tip. Winking at him, Paul said, "I won't tell if you don't."

The driver winked back and said, *"Bol'shoye spacibo."*

Lying flat out on the bed, Sam was obviously in a great deal of pain. Paul helped him out of his shirt and trousers. The bruise had turned uglier and the area of the break was swollen to twice its normal size. Paul decided to make one more try.

"Sam, this is a dangerous situation you're getting into. Let me see if I can get a doctor to come around and look at your leg. I'll be right here all the time he's in the room."

"Damn it, Paul, I'm not going to let any Russian doctor touch me out here in the boonies. So let's not quibble any more about that. Just give me a couple of your aspirin and a big drink out of our vodka bottle, and then go see how soon we can get started back to Moscow."

Sam had been highly decorated in the Korean War, and Paul knew he was courageous and that he meant what he said about no Russian doctor. He knew too that the next twelve hours were going to be difficult ones for Sam. So he gave him three aspirin and poured a half tumbler of vodka and stayed in the room until Sam had downed both.

Then he went down to the lobby and explained the situation to the Inturist representative. She listened in obvious disbelief—Russian female officials are determined obstructionists and they're obvious about it—but she agreed to contact the airport (read KGB) to see what she could do. "I will let you know in two or three hours," she said.

"That's no good," Paul replied, "this is an emergency. Please contact the authorities and explain that I must get my friend back to Moscow as soon as possible."

Paul went out front and found the "taxi" driver who had brought Sam and him back to the hotel earlier. He had apparently made his report and was now back on surveillance duty. Paul explained that he and his companion would probably be leaving for the airport within a couple of hours, and asked that he stand by for them. Since he was responsible for surveillance of the Americans, he agreed at once to do as Paul asked.

Paul suddenly realized he hadn't had any food since a hard-boiled-egg breakfast early that morning (eating in hotel dining rooms or restaurants while traveling in the Soviet Union made for a no-win situation. A simple breakfast could take an hour to be served. The American travelers believed the KGB wanted the dining room and restaurant help to stall for as long as possible. The more time the travelers spent at meals, the less time they would have on the street for observation. So the Americans carried "iron rations" for breakfast and lunch. They usually used the hotel dining rooms for dinner.) So Paul went back into the hotel and found the maître d.' He ordered a simple meal, and the maître d' expressed astonishment that he wanted it in less than an hour. Paul explained they had a plane to catch, and added five ten-ruble notes to the explanation.

Then he went to check on Sam. He found him asleep with the vodka bottle almost empty. Dinner came in fifteen minutes. On the tray was a .75 liter bottle of premium vodka that Paul thought Sam (and he) could use as they moved in the direction of Moscow. He woke Sam, and they had a couple of stiff drinks before they started on dinner. Sam was obviously in pain, but the vodka helped and he made no complaints.

Dinner over, Paul went down to check with the Inturist representative. Almost reluctantly, she said she had found space for Paul and Sam on a flight that would leave Alma Ata in about an hour and connect with a flight that would put them into Moscow around midnight. That was great news. Paul speculated that he and Sam were making more trouble for the local KGB than they wanted, and the word was out: "Get those guys out of town."

The KGB driver (who apparently knew their new schedule as well as the Inturist rep) came to the room to remind them it was time to go to the airport and to help them with their luggage. He and Paul supported Sam down into the lobby and out to their "taxi." Sam seemed to be doing remarkably well for a man with a broken leg. Paul figured it was a combination of grit—Sam had plenty of that—and vodka.

The flight to Tbilisi was uneventful. Sam fell asleep almost as soon as the wheels came up. Waiting for their connecting flight, Paul telephoned the embassy duty officer from Tbilisi, explained what was going on, and asked that a driver meet them at Sheremetyevo Airport when they arrived. Just getting through to Moscow from Tbilisi was a great victory, and he and Sam had a couple of drinks from the vodka bottle Paul was carrying in his attaché case to celebrate. They solemnly agreed it was an occasion equal to Alexander Graham Bell's first words over the telephone: "Mr. Watson, come here, I want you."

Sam slept most of the way from Tbilisi, while Paul struggled to stay awake. The plane was filled with Georgian farmers carrying fresh produce—mostly on their laps—to Moscow, where they would get the highest price. One grizzled old man in a long sheepskin coat had a goat on a tether. The goat stood in the center aisle, and Paul remembers thinking the goat was like the rest of the passengers. He wasn't wearing a seat belt. The goat bleated all the way to Moscow. Paul needed help in staying awake, and he was thankful for the racket.

The duty officer at the embassy was thoughtful enough to let me know that Paul and Sam were arriving from Tbilisi. He called Sam's wife as well, and we were there to welcome them home. Both of the drivers boarded the aircraft to help Sam off. When I saw Paul, I figured he might need as much help as Sam did.

"Paul, you're drunk," I said, "and it looks like Sam's drunker than you are."

"Yeah, Florence," he replied, "it's been an interesting day. Sam's drunk and I'm happy he is. He is one tough bastard. He's put down a whole bottle of aspirin and most of a liter of vodka. His leg is broken and he never once said, 'It hurts.'"

Paul fell asleep just as soon as he climbed into the car for the long ride home. So there was no opportunity to talk about what had happened to Sam and him, and to find out why they were *both* drunk. Sam I could understand, but Paul rarely allowed himself to get bent out of shape. So why this time?

Back in our apartment, Paul sat down on the bed and fell asleep again as I was trying to get his shirt off. I managed to get him into his pajamas and put his head down on the pillow.

"Paul," I asked, "why are you so drunk? What happened?"

His eyes snapped open and for just a moment he looked lucid.

"Well, Florence, all I can tell you is the KGB made me do it." This said, he gave a secret little smile and lapsed back into sleep.

Moscow was a gray and cheerless city, and most of the diplomats had little to do. So they entertained each other frequently. American Embassy personnel worked harder and longer than I have ever seen elsewhere, and they needed relief now and then from the somber environment in Moscow. So all of us entertained and were entertained as an antidote to depression. There were many receptions, formal and informal dinner parties and, now and then, dancing. That was when the host usually brought out the good champagne. So there was *some* compensation for the island of isolation that was Moscow.

One of the simpler means of entertainment for the Americans was a film-showing at home. Films were brought into our embassy from Germany weekly, and most were new, good films. Paul and I entertained this way about twice a month, and found that many of the diplomats from the smaller embassies—and the British and French as well—enjoyed the films and appreciated being invited. One day, as we were putting together a list of people we wanted to invite for a film showing, Paul pulled one of his slates from his

Paul in Zürs, Austria (1963).

pocket and wrote on it the name of a couple I didn't know. (When we were in London, Paul bought a half-dozen child's toys that are made of a carbon-like paper sheet that is covered with clear plastic. Paul carried two of these slates and two pencils wherever he went in the embassy, including the ambassador's office. When he had written his message and it had been read, he simply lifted the plastic sheet and it disappeared. At night, Paul locked his slates in his safe.)

I wrote on my slate, "I don't know them."

Paul replied, "Okay, I'll do it."

That's the kind of thing that used to drive me nuts in Moscow. There were literally hundreds of cryptic and unfinished messages between Paul and myself, and there was nothing to do except carry on.

The couple came as invited, and I noted that Paul took pains to seat himself next to the husband on the sofa. I naturally wondered what was going on, but I turned on the projector and turned off the lights.

When our guests had left that evening, I found a yellow pad and wrote, "Now what was that all about?"

Paul just grinned, shrugged and threw up his hands as if he had to protect himself from me. Not only didn't I get an answer, but I had to burn my message in an ash tray and flush the ashes down the toilet.

A few weeks later, Paul told me he had invited the couple back for a film, and the men sat next to one another again. This time I didn't question the invitation or the seating. It was not until Paul retired from the agency that I found out "what that was all about."

The young diplomat had been recruited in his capital when the CIA station there learned of his upcoming assignment to Moscow. He had agreed to respond to an American who would pass to him in writing or orally an agreed-upon password or "parole."

Paul skiing at Zürs, Austria.

Paul had received from Langley a cone-shaped metal cylinder that was to be placed in the ground at a designated location. The cylinder was hollow and had a screw top, so that a message could be hidden inside, and was sharply pointed at the end so that it could be "planted" in the ground. Paul passed the tube, together with the password and instructions, to the young diplomat the first time he visited.

Paul wanted confirmation that the cylinder had been planted, so he invited the couple back. This time he was surprised to get the cylinder *back*. There was an explanatory note inside. Briefly, it said that the young man had not carried out the mission because he was under surveillance, and he didn't think this kind of thing was good for his health or career anyway.

When Paul informed Langley of what happened, and offered to get the job done with one of his own people, Langley said no, send the cylinder back. He did. It sat in a safe for a week or so, and was then sent to the Technical Services Division for a complete checkout. The word came back that it was *radioactive*. A small chunk of radioactive material had been implanted in the screwtop,

Paul (far left) at Zürs.

sufficient to give off a signal that could be picked up out to a mile away from the cylinder.

Langley knew that the KGB had a team of expert safecrackers. They also knew that the team routinely made the rounds of the smaller, poorly guarded embassies, opening safes just to see what they might find of interest. Langley speculated that the team had done a routine break-in and found the cylinder. Not knowing what to expect, they had doctored the cylinder and put surveillance on the diplomat. If he had gone on to plant it where CIA wanted it, the KGB would have been able to track it without difficulty.

As Paul told me a long time after all this transpired, he went back over what had happened, and he calculated he'd had the radioactive cylinder in his pants pocket and under his pillow for a total of more than ten hours. He could live with the pillow; it was his pants pocket he was worried about.

He said, "Jesus, Florence, I had that damned thing resting right next to my privates for like six hours. That could have made me impotent."

At last I had this macho person right where I wanted him. I paused, relishing the moment, and said, "Well, it almost did." The expression on his face was something I'll never forget.

Paul took me down to GUM one Sunday afternoon. We parked the embassy Ford a couple of blocks away, and he explained during our walk that there was nothing for me to do except to be there with him. Sunday is the average Muscovite's shopping day, and there were thousands of shoppers loose in GUM that day. We struggled through the solid mass of people to a public telephone, where Paul made a call while I stood by. We knew that two scruffy-looking characters had followed us from the car, and were now right on our backs. One of them pushed against me and drove his elbow into my ribs. I gave him my nastiest glare, but he just snickered. When Paul rejoined me, I told him what happened. He asked me which one had done the shoving, and I pointed him out.

We were being carried along by the crowd, with our two surveillants within a few feet of us. Paul moved me around patiently until we were behind them. We could see them jumping up over the heads of the shoppers to try to locate us. We were caught up in a tide of bodies, and so were the surveillants. Paul moved forward and deliberately stepped on the heel of the man who had shoved me, almost taking his shoe off. There was no reaction. When Paul did it a second time, the Russian stiffened. I jerked at Paul's sleeve, wanting him to stop this childish behavior, but he was determined. He stamped hard on the Russian's heel again, this time causing him to stumble. The Russian turned and tried to stand still against the press of the crowd. As the mass of bodies ebbed and flowed around them, Paul and the Russian stood there, toe to toe, glaring at one another, fists clenched. Finally, the Russian was pulled away by his comrade, and we continued on our way out. The thought came to me that the long years of Cold War confrontation had narrowed down to less than a minute when one Russian and one American tried to face each other down in GUM. I figured we were lucky there had been no fireworks.

Paul apologized as we walked back to the car. "I'm sorry, Florence, that was a dumb trick. But those guys broke the rules. It's okay for them to *be* there, Christ knows in this country they'll *always* be there. But it's not permitted for them to push you around or try to intimidate you. Those are no-nos. Today they stepped over the line, and I lost my head. I'm sorry."

Looking back over our time there, I didn't resent Paul's not keeping me any better informed about what he was trying to do in Moscow. I had reservations about Paul's leaving the Navy for CIA because I realized he was moving into a world where there were *secrets*. With Paul, it was never secrets for secrets' sake. His mind just doesn't work that way. I knew there was a dark side to what he was doing, and not even my love and affection for him would be permitted to shine a light into that darkness. But it was enough for me that we were there in enemy territory together, and every now and then I could help him.

9. Trouble

ARLY IN 1964, Paul received word that our tour in Moscow would end in June or July. That would give us two and one-half years in the Big City, and for me that was enough.

About a month later, Paul met with David Murphy, the new chief of the Soviet Russia Division, somewhere in Western Europe. The conversation went something like this:

"Well, Paul, what would you like to do after you finish up in Moscow?"

"I've been thinking about putting in for the National War College."

"You can't do that. You're a spy. Spies don't go to schools like that and get exposed."

"Okay, what do you suggest as an alternative?"

"I'd like you to come on as my deputy in the SR Division. Would you like that?"

Paul said, "Hell, yes," and that was that.

In March of 1964, Paul went off to Zürs in the Austrian Alps for a ski vacation. He asked me to go with him, but I'm much better at après ski than I am at downhill, so I demurred. He'd played hockey with the embassy team all winter to get his legs in shape, and he was in excellent health when he left.

When I next saw him, which was in a neurological clinic in

111

Innsbruck, Paul went back over events as they occurred, so I had a coherent story. It seems he suffered a bad fall on his first day in Zürs, but he managed to get up and make his way down the mountain, congratulating himself that he didn't break a leg or snap an ankle bone. He had a headache for a couple of days, but aspirin helped, so he didn't give it much thought. Then he went very high with a group that was skiing down the reverse side of the mountain to the neighboring village of Lech. About halfway down, he found it increasingly difficult to make the swinging turns and felt a numbness in his left arm and leg.

The instructor leading the group came back to him and said, "Paul, you look terrible. I don't think you should try to go any further. Please wait here. There's a phone a couple of hundred meters down the slope, and I'll call for our search and rescue people to come up and take you down in a sled. I know you'll enjoy that."

Paul didn't argue. He sat in the snow and watched the instructor become an ever-smaller black spot on a vast white landscape as he plummeted down the mountain. "What the hell's wrong with me?" he thought. By now his arm and leg had grown a lot more numb.

The rescue team arrived promptly, and strapped him into place on a kind of toboggan, which they would control with ropes secured to the sides. They tried to get Paul to lie down, but he insisted on sitting. Once they got underway and gathered speed, Paul said it was the best ride he ever had.

They took him straight to the village doctor. Zürs in 1964 was a tiny farm village high in the Vorarlberg. There was only one young doctor, and his expertise lay in setting broken bones. By now Paul was convinced there was something wrong with his head. The doctor examined him carefully and asked about his symptoms. Always the paranoid professional, Paul said he wanted a urinalysis and a blood check. The doctor said he had no means to do the tests, and suggested Paul get ready to be moved to Innsbruck. A world-renowned neurologist had a clinic there, and "Herr Professor" could care for Paul much better than he could. Paul argued a while about not wanting to mess up his vacation and then fell asleep. When he woke, the doctor was on the phone with "Herr Professor," and Paul heard the words "possible brain tumor."

When he heard that, Paul didn't argue any more. He was taken down by ambulance, still in ski clothes. He slept all the way down. In Innsbruck, he was taken to a scatter of gloomy-looking dark brick buildings near the center of the city. He was greeted at the door by a tall, gaunt figure in a long white coat—the professor— and two nuns in habit, great white collars and enormous starched white headgear.

Again Paul asked for urine and blood tests. The professor replied there were more important tests that had to be done right away. As in Zürs, all the conversation was in German. Paul knew how to curse in German, and he used some strong language with the professor once the nuns were out of earshot, but he never did get the tests he wanted. Paul was convinced he'd been drugged— with what or why he had no idea—but he couldn't tell the professor that without prompting a whole battery of questions he was not prepared to deal with. Unmoved, the professor went ahead with his tests, some of which nearly blew the top of Paul's head off. But he found himself liking the tall, ramrod-straight professor, and his confidence began to build.

Paul was not permitted to telephone, so he asked the professor to call his "friend"—actually the chief of station—in the embassy in Vienna to tell him he was here in Innsbruck. I received a call from Vienna, and was on the first plane I could get out of Moscow. I called Susan in Switzerland and asked her to meet me at the clinic. I arrived in Innsbruck in the early morning hours, and was at the clinic when they opened the doors. The professor met me and took me to Paul. He looked terribly pale and weak. The nuns were hovering over him, straightening the bedclothes and punching the pillows. He tried to give me a big smile and pretend this was a piece of cake, but there was no question he was in trouble. Susan arrived a few hours after I did, and he made an effort to sit up in bed and make jokes. I could see her being there was very good for him.

I spoke with the professor, and he said they were mystified. All the tests were negative for any serious disturbance in the brain. Yet Paul had symptoms that pointed to some kind of abnormality. He wanted to keep Paul there for a while to see if they couldn't isolate the problem and help him. I agreed he should stay.

That first morning, in addition to the two nuns, there was a short, wiry man standing guard over Paul. Paul introduced him as Karl Oberguckenberger—a name I shall never forget—and told me he'd practically handcuffed himself to Paul's bed ever since his first day in the clinic. Paul said he was a "mountain man," very much like our mountain men in Kentucky or Tennessee, and he'd apparently decided he was going to protect Paul from the terrible things the professor and his associates might want to do to him. A few days later, I watched him bring Paul back on a stretcher from one of the tests. Weighing much less than Paul, he lifted him with ease and placed him gently back in bed.

Paul hadn't had any food for a long time, so Susan and I went out on the town after the best lunch we could find. We were both troubled to see him so weak, but we didn't want to admit it to each other, so we concentrated on the food. Austrian food is lovingly prepared and hearty. We came back with enough for four. Paul had some, and he insisted that Karl join us.

Paul was a patient in the clinic for three weeks. He grew stronger every day and regained the full use of his left arm and leg. He'd lost a lot of weight and was still quite weak, but we were happy that the professor pronounced him well enough to travel. CIA did not want Paul in the clinic at all, and Paul's "friend" in Vienna, on instructions from Langley, called every day to try to get him out. They simply didn't understand how sick he was.

The chief of station in Vienna sent a young officer with a very large Mercedes to take us to the airport in Munich. We wanted to fly directly to Moscow, but Langley and the cover organization insisted that Paul check in at the Air Force Hospital in Wiesbaden, where American doctors could evaluate his condition. As we rolled out of the driveway, the professor, standing in the doorway tall and straight in his long white coat, waved a solemn goodbye. The two sisters stood next to him, waving also. The younger one, Elisabet, threw us a kiss. Karl stood at the side of the drive weeping, the tears rolling down his cheeks.

The professor had written a five-page synopsis—in German, of course—of his findings in testing Paul over three weeks. We gave it to the Air Force doctors when we arrived at Wiesbaden, but they weren't interested. Paul offered to help translate it into English, but they still weren't interested. Their instant diagnosis was that Paul had suffered a stroke *and* a heart attack. That was before they did any tests. Having arrived at this intuitive diagnosis, they then worked backward, trying hard to prove it.

They put Paul through a battery of stress tests—and others— that would have killed him if he'd had a heart attack. He gained a little strength each day and, after about a week of this, we went together to the commanding officer of the hospital. His position was that Paul should be "air-evaced" to the States as soon as possible. Paul said he did not agree. He needed to return to Moscow. The debate went on for four days, until the general finally relented and released Paul from the hospital. All the while the Air Force doctors were poking and prodding at him, Paul said to me, "Florence, I walked into Moscow upright—I'm not, by God, leaving it on a stretcher."

We flew back to Moscow the day after Paul was released. There was an Air Force doctor resident in the embassy, a fine young man, and we checked in with him right after we arrived. He had heard all manner of wild rumors out of Wiesbaden, and he was delighted to see Paul up and moving around.

Difficult as it was for all of us, there was a ludicrous aspect to Paul's confinement. The cover people were talking to Langley and the chief of station in Vienna daily about Paul's stay in an Austrian clinic. They didn't want him there, they wanted him in an American *military* hospital. CIA was equally concerned. So the chief of station, at Langley's urging, would call the professor daily and tell him they were sending an airplane to air-evacuate Paul to the Air Force Hospital in Wiesbaden—or all the way back to the States.

The professor spoke a little English, and his routine reply was that Paul was not ready to leave the clinic. When he was well enough to go, he'd call the chief of station and let him know. The COS was an old friend and wanted to do the right thing for Paul, but he was caught in the middle.

What made the whole business bizarre was that there had been a terrible plane crash at the Innsbruck Airport a couple of months earlier. As a result of the accident, the airport had been closed, and it was still closed while CIA and the cover organization were bugging the professor about air-evacuating Paul out of Innsbruck.

We stayed in Moscow until June. Paul went to the office every day, but he was far from recovered. He went to Lenin Stadium early every morning to walk and jog on the track. He pushed himself a little further every day. I watched him coming out of it, and I was relieved. But I knew he was not yet well.

10. Trouble of a Different Kind

HEN WE returned to Washington, the CIA doctors suggested that Paul spend at least a week at the Bethesda Naval Medical Center. Paul was disappointed but agreed to cooperate. He discussed his symptoms with the Navy doctors, and they went over him with a fine tooth comb. They had the professor's report translated, and they asked him a lot of questions about it. Some of them knew the professor by reputation.

Paul was an in-patient at the Medical Center for almost three weeks, while I stayed at a hotel nearby. I could see that he was growing impatient with the confinement, and it was beginning to make him short-tempered. He had now spent a total of eight weeks in hospitals, and the doctors still hadn't told him what was wrong. Finally, the Navy and CIA doctors told us that what had caused Paul's temporary paralysis and weakness did not come from something *inside* his brain or body, it was caused by an *external* force of some kind, a drug or a blow perhaps. They added that they believed he would make a complete recovery in three to six months.

They made an accurate prognosis. About six months after we left Moscow, all of the physical weakness and depression simply faded away. He had regained his strength, and his head was working as it used to.

One of the first things Paul did after he reported in at Langley was to ask one of the research assistants in the Soviet Russia Division to check the records for Soviet travel in and out of Austria for one month before and after he was in Zürs. The check revealed that General Oleg Gribanov, head of the Second Chief Directorate of the KGB, known to be a talented and aggressive officer, had arrived in St. Anton, only a few miles from Zürs, a week before Paul arrived in Zürs. Taking into account how unusual it was for a senior KGB general to travel to Austria to ski, and what had happened to him, Paul found it difficult to accept Gribanov's presence in St. Anton as a coincidence.

When Paul reported in to the SR Division, he was well and ready to go to work. He made the rounds of the various components of the division for briefings and thought they were grossly inadequate. He had been deliberately isolated from ongoing SR operations while he was in Moscow, so he asked for files and briefings to bring him up to speed on what was going on. He encountered delays and evasions. He had to wonder whether this was routine in the SR Division, or if the strange practice applied only to him.

Then, late one evening, a cable came to him for clearance that didn't seem right. So he went down to the branch that originated the cable and asked for the backup. It developed that the evidence to support the warning that was going out to just about every CIA station in the world was a conversation that had taken place between a CIA station chief and a KGB *rezident* (the equivalent of a station chief). The conversation had been recorded, and there was a transcript. It seemed to Paul that the transcript ran directly counter to what was being reported to the world, so he said:

"Peter, these things don't match. What actually happened is the opposite of what is being reported. Is this the only evidence we have?"

"Yeah, Paul, and let me give you a little advice. Don't make waves. Release the cable. That's exactly the way Dave wants it to go out."

"I can't do that, Peter. I'll talk to Dave about it in the morning."

"It's your ass."

•

Paul was in David Murphy's office early the following morning. The conversation went something like this:

"Paul, I understand you refused to release a cable last night that I asked the branch to send out."

"That's right."

"Why?"

"Well, I didn't know anything about what was being reported, so I went down to the branch looking for information to support the cable. I read a transcript of a conversation, the gist of which was exactly the opposite of what was being reported to the field."

"Yeah, but Peter says he told you I wanted the cable to go just that way."

"That's true, he did. But I'm not signing off on anything that's obviously misleading."

"But I wanted that cable to go last night."

"Well, Dave, here it is. Why don't you release it?"

"Paul, it's beginning to look like you don't belong on my team. Let's just say it hasn't worked out."

"Dave, if this is the way you do your business, I know I don't belong on your team."

So Paul left the SR Division and moved over to the Western European Division, where he very quickly learned more about worldwide Soviet operations than he had in SR. There was something terribly wrong about that, but Paul couldn't come up with the answer. He was happy enough, but he realized he'd lost an opportunity, as Deputy Chief of SR Division, to take on some of the most challenging tasks the Clandestine Service faces.

About a year after he joined the WE Division, there was a reorganization within the Clandestine Service and it became the expanded European Division. The division chief sent a memorandum to the chief of the Clandestine Service, nominating Paul as the chief of operations of the European Division. A few weeks later, the memo came back. Written in pencil on the margin were the words "Excellent choice. I concur."

A couple of weeks after that, Paul was in his office late on a Friday evening releasing cables when the division chief came in and told him Tom Karamessines, the deputy chief of the Clandestine Service, wanted to see him. "Now?" Paul asked. "It's almost seven o'clock."

"He said now. Forget the cables, I'll take care of them."

It didn't take long to find out what Tom K. wanted.

"Paul, we've been talking about you this afternoon, the Director (Richard Helms) and I. We've decided to send you down to the Farm as the representative of the Clandestine Service."

Those two sentences, so casually pronounced, in Paul's judgment sounded the death knell of his career. Now he *knew* there was something terribly wrong, and he had to find out what it was. Now what had happened to his job as deputy chief of the SR Division began to fit a pattern. He'd have to save that for later; right now he had to try to change Tom K.'s mind about the Farm.

"The Farm? I don't know anything about training. I don't belong down there."

"Ah, but you do. We very much need someone down there with the kind of operational experience you had in Moscow. You can motivate our trainees to play a role in the kind of operations you ran in Moscow, the most difficult ones. You're the right man for the job alright. We're lucky to have you." These saccharine, laudatory comments were totally out of character for Tom K. He was a man who dealt in cold, hard fact. Paul knew that and knew that he was being snowed. But it appeared that Tom had set himself on a course, and was not to be deterred. "And we'd like to have you down there quickly," Tom added.

"Quickly? What do you mean by quickly?"

"Within a week. They have a new training cycle beginning next week, and we'd like to see you on the job before then."

So far as Paul was concerned, he was having a conversation with a madman. But Tom K. was speaking for the chief of the service and the Director, and Paul had to assume he would not be speaking these mindless words without their backing. So what was going on, first in the SR Division, and now at the highest reach of the service? What did they know that they weren't telling him?

Paul stayed there for an hour longer, arguing and resisting, trying to provoke the truth out of Tom K. Finally, he asked if the

Director would accept his refusal to go to the Farm. Tom K., no newcomer to this kind of a tussle with a recalcitrant officer, shot back, "Only if it is accompanied by your resignation."

This Paul could not bring himself to do. He had too many years and too much sweat invested, and Tom K. knew it. When he had exhausted all his arguments, and Tom K. never budged, Paul capitulated, but not before he extracted a promise that his tour at the Farm would not exceed two years, and that he would be reassigned as a chief of station.

Paul did not tell me that evening that we were going to the Farm. The conversation he'd had with Tom K. was so odd that he hoped it would simply evaporate over the weekend like a bad dream. So there was no point in giving me bad news if we were back to status quo on Monday morning. He couldn't believe management was serious about turning him into a zero. Why would they want to do that?

When Paul finally gave me the news—he had arranged for us to have three drinks before dinner that evening—I was crushed. We had bought a lovely old house in Chevy Chase, and I was knee deep in decorating it from attic to basement. Susan was back in a good American school, and doing well. We had been assured Paul would be at Langley for three years this time, and here we were moving again. So it was not a happy time for any of us.

We spent two years at the Farm, living in a tiny house that would have almost fit into our Chevy Chase living room. Like General Halftrack in the *Beetle Bailey* comic strip, who sits in Camp Swampy and waits for a message from the Pentagon, Paul waited, day by day, for a message that would say, "Come back, it's all a mistake." General Halftrack's message never comes, and neither did Paul's.

Not wanting to sit on his hands for two years, Paul went through the entire training cycle for the junior officer trainees (JOTs) with two different classes. This included paramilitary exercises and four days spent in the Panama jungle for survival training. He submitted a twelve-page evaluation of the training to Tom K. when he left the Farm. But it was like the word had gone out

Paul in the Panama jungle (1968).

by Clandestine Service jungle telegraph that he had leprosy. Visitors from Langley, some of them old friends and associates, were obvious in their determination to have absolutely nothing to do with him. It was a time of great humiliation for Paul. He tried to treat it lightly, but I knew it was eating at him that the fine rep-

Paul (center of boat, standing) in training
in Panama jungle.

utation he'd worked so hard for was being so casually destroyed.
He returned to Tom K. many times during those years, trying to
provoke an explanation for what had happened. If only Tom would
lay it out for him, he was confident he could clear up any misun-
derstanding. Tom pooh-poohed all of this. There were no misun-
derstandings, Paul's assignment to the Farm was routine, he was
doing fine.

Precisely two years after our arrival at the Farm, Paul was in

Tom K.'s office to discuss his next assignment. He felt he had to exert what little pressure he could bring to bear on Tom and the Director if he was ever going to emerge from the morass he was in. Tom K. had by now moved up to become the chief of the Service.

"Ah, yes, Paul, I promised you a station when you completed your work at the Farm. You've done well there, I haven't forgotten my promise, I've kept you in mind. I discussed your report with the Director only a few days ago. We've made a choice I'm sure you'll like."

"That's great. Which station are we talking about?"

"Well, you'll be our new chief of station in Port of Spain, Trinidad."

The expression on Paul's face apparently gave Tom reason to hurry along in his explanation of the assignment. "The Director views the situation in the Caribbean as critical just now for a variety of reasons. He is concerned over recent developments in that part of the world, close to our own shores, and he wants a good, reliable man there to keep pace with happenings throughout the region and keep us advised. I've recommended you for the job, and Dick Helms has enthusiastically concurred."

Paul was incredulous. He had visited Trinidad once in 1948, when he was on the aircraft carrier *Leyte*. He found the Caribbean like a string of pearls, each island different, elegant, sensuous and delicately beautiful in its own way. But the focus is on tourism, rum (both the making and the drinking), sex and steel band music. He had toiled for years to learn his trade in Soviet and Eastbloc operations. What would he find to do in Trinidad?

Paul finally found his voice. "Tom, I can't believe this is happening. Is Trinidad the only post you can offer me? If that's it, please don't double talk me about how important it is. Just tell me why you're working so hard to destroy me. What the hell is going on?"

Over another hour, Paul got little more than Tom's routine, soothing replies. They did not soothe him at all. When he left, he told Tom he wanted a few days to think about the assignment in order to decide whether to take it or resign. Tom did not urge him to stay on. He said only that if Paul chose to stay on, Trinidad was his next assignment.

Paul went directly from Tom's office to the office of Howard Osborn, then Director of Security. Paul and Howard were friends from the SR Division, and Paul was puzzled by Howard's silence on what had been happening to him. So he carried his frustration and anger directly from Tom's office to Howard's. He was fortunate enough to find him in and between appointments.

"Howard, what the hell is going on? First I am wrenched out of a good job and sent into isolation at the Farm for two years. Now Tom tells me I'm to be the Agency's Caribbean watchdog. The Caribbean, for Christ's sake. Did you know about this?"

"Yeah, I'd heard. The appointment was announced at yesterday's staff meeting with the Director."

"Then it's for real, and Tom's not just trying to scare the spit out of me. Do I look like the kind of fellow who belongs in Trinidad?"

"Well," Howard said, leaning way back in his chair and placing his fingertips together, all the while avoiding Paul's eyes, "It's kind of like assigning Dick Helms to run the incinerator. You know he'll do a good job, but it's overkill."

Paul stayed with Howard until his next appointment, trying to elicit from him any insight he might want to provide into what lay behind these bizarre events. He struck out completely. Howard laughed and joked a lot, but it was obvious he wasn't going to get involved.

Now Paul knew that even his close friends in the Agency could not be counted on in this crisis. There was nowhere to go except out or to an island paradise, to languish there like some remittance man.

In the end, Paul caved in and went off to Trinidad. We spent hours going over the pros and cons, trying to decide whether the indignity of the assignment could be counterbalanced by what the future might hold. Paul was by then fifty years old, our daughter was just entering college, we were about as deeply in debt as the average American family, and he could not conceive of anyone in the "outside" employment market clamoring after a middle-aged spy.

So we went to Trinidad and stayed for four years. Four years! Paul thought we should stay until it was safe to come home. He knew it wasn't safe to come home earlier because he had *some* friends left, and he tested the line periodically.

When Paul went off to Trinidad, we had no idea where we might find housing. So Paul went first, and I stayed behind to arrange for the shipment of our household effects and the dogs, by now a poodle named Max and a cocker spaniel we called Huckleberry. Susan was in college and would stay put.

Paul found a large, open, airy house in the center of the city, secluded and yet convenient to everything. It was perfect for our needs. And, better than that, he hired Yvonne, who was to be our cook for all the time we lived in Port of Spain. Yvonne admitted to

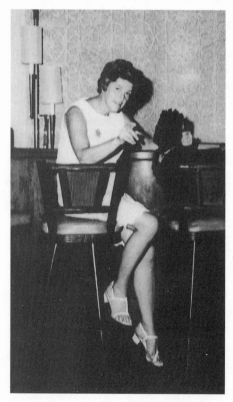

Florence with Max in Trinidad (1969).

sixty when we first knew her, but she was alert, spry and getting better at preparing the food of the islands every day we knew her. Huckleberry was more interested in food than breathing, and he glued himself to Yvonne from day one, spending the nights with her where she slept behind the house.

The embassy in Port of Spain was a tiny one. There was no place to hide, so Paul did his best to make it look like he belonged there. He was fortunate to have two ambassadors during his time there who cooperated generously in the cover problem. We became friendly with both couples and still try to spend time with one whenever we go east on our periodic visits with Susan and our grandsons. We think of them as good friends, and it is always a pleasure to see them.

Paul didn't want simply to vacation in Trinidad, so, when he got his feet on the ground, he began to look for opportunities to recruit new sources. He realized, sadly enough, that none of these was going to tell him what went on behind Kremlin doors, or even what Castro was plotting. He simply had to accept that, while he could do pretty much as he wanted, the only game in town was the government of Trinidad and Tobago and that of the other Caribbean islands.

The Trinidadian army led a revolt during our time there. Two junior officers took control of the army for a brief period of great uncertainty. The normally placid, fun-loving Trinidadians rioted in the downtown streets and marched through the more affluent neighborhoods chanting, "Down with the government. Death to traitors. No more white rule." Paul and the labor attaché drove downtown to see for themselves what was happening. The Trinidadians were jumping in the streets "higher than Watusis." There was widespread looting. A crowd gathered around the car and began rocking it, hoping to turn it over. Paul was finally able to get clear of the crowd by racing the engine and threatening to plow into the solid mass of bodies. When Paul and the attaché returned to the embassy and reported, the ambassador unloaded on them—as he should have—and said he was pleased they'd satisfied their curiosity.

It was a mess. Families we knew sent wives and children off to Barbados, and the men armed themselves. I stayed in our home despite Paul's protestations.

But even with all of that, it was a rebellion Trinidad-style—and the Trinidadians have lots of style. Many of the rioters were accompanied by steel bands on flatbed trucks as they moved through the streets jumping with joy. The army base backed up to the sea, so it was not difficult for the police, who remained loyal, to bottle up the mutineers, preventing them from breaking out to tear up the city. But the police continued to permit trucks loaded with food and supplies—and lots of rum—to pass through the main gate of the base, so that the seditious officers and men would not go hungry—or thirsty. So it was a kind of "chocolate soldier" rebellion, but one that could have turned ugly at any time.

About six months after we arrived in Port of Spain, Paul had a "walk-in." A young student at the University of the West Indies in St. Augustine came into the consulate asking to see an intelligence officer. When he and Paul were together in a small conference room, the student said he was an admirer of the United States and wanted some day to go there to live. There were things happening on the St. Augustine campus that he didn't like, and he believed Paul would be interested in what he knew.

What he knew was a matter of much interest to Paul. The CIA was concerned about the radicalization of the Caribbean peoples by a movement that was born and had flourished elsewhere. The student said he could identify the leaders of the movement on the campus. He added that they wanted to bring down the present Trinidadian government and replace it with one that would be anti-U.S. and anti-West. Since there was considerable American and Western investment in Trinidad and Tobago, this sounded like an ominous development. When Paul asked if he would join the movement and work for the U.S. from the inside, the student readily agreed. He refused Paul's offer of a modest salary but agreed to accept payment for expenses.

It was clear that this was not your run-of-the-mill young Trinidadian chasing after "fête" and sex and rum. He was a tall, gaunt fellow, humorless, lugubrious-looking, apparently as devoted to a widowed mother as he was to the democratic cause. He would require special handling and, as they went along together, he got it. He proved to be a valuable asset in an area of considerable interest to the U.S. at the time. He remained an active source for all the time we were in Trinidad. He wanted to emigrate to the States, but his mother would not relocate and he would not leave her.

Paul looked hard for a year or so for a source that could tell him what was happening inside the Trinidad and Tobago government and what the leadership planned for the future. He took his time doing this because he wanted to be sure he settled on someone who would have the right access. Several American companies had large investments in Trinidad, and an administration that might want to expropriate property or otherwise threaten free trade was anathema to American business. The National Security Council had a standing requirement to be advised *in advance* of the possibility that such a government might come to power in Trinidad.

After a downtown lunch with friends one day, Paul stopped in the restaurant's men's room. As he stood at a urinal, he felt a presence behind him, and an envelope was deposited in the wash basin next to the urinal. He turned quickly, wanting to see who was in the room with him, but all he saw was the back of a stocky figure disappearing out the door. He checked the adjoining hallways, but there was no one there. He went into one of the stalls, took down his pants, and sat there reading the note. It contained detailed, convoluted instructions for making "secret" contact with the writer, who alleged he had information of great value to the U.S. Paul thought it was written by someone who had seen too many television shows about kidnappings and ransom payments.

The instructions called for Paul to meet the writer at about dusk at a specific location on the abandoned U.S. Naval Base at Macqueripe, outside Port of Spain. There were two additional sites on the base given, where Paul was instructed to pause, apparently so that the writer could identify him and his car, and ascertain he was alone.

Paul gave it some thought and decided it was worth trying. But he put a baseball bat under the car's passenger seat and left his money and anything that could identify him in the wall safe in our bedroom, just in case someone was planning a nice surprise. He concluded that if anyone wanted to rob or kidnap him, there were less involved ways to get the job done.

The stocky man (I will call him Rajiv, which of course was not his name) was waiting for him where he said he would be. He climbed into the car and they went for a drive around the base. Rajiv did the talking and Paul the listening. He told Paul his job gave him excellent natural access (it was obvious that it did) to middle- and high-level governmental officials. In addition, he had confirmable information on the turmoil inside the government that resulted from the coup attempt.

Rajiv said he had decided to join forces with Paul because his employer gave him a pittance as salary and refused to reimburse him for the paid sources he'd developed in the government. Rajiv was running out of money fast, and he wanted Paul to help him keep his sources going and permit him to have a good time with what was left over. That sounded very Trinidadian, and tended to confirm Rajiv's *bona fides* in Paul's eyes. The amount he asked for sounded reasonable, and Paul said he thought his headquarters would authorize him to go along with Rajiv for a trial period of, say, three months. If Rajiv produced what he promised, they would make a more permanent arrangement.

Rajiv asked Paul to meet him in a week for a drink "in a safe place," and gave him the address. Paul got enough biographic information from Rajiv to submit a trace request and a request for a provisional security clearance. There were no traces and Paul received a conditional clearance to work with Rajiv.

When Paul went to the address Rajiv gave him, he found a small Victorian-style house in bad repair. The doorbell was answered by an overweight, very black lady in a ratty kimono who showed him into the parlor, where Rajiv was waiting. As soon as Paul was seated, a shapely young girl, clad only in bra and panties, came in with a pitcher of rum punch and two glasses. The girl looked like "something straight out of *Playboy* magazine."

"Jesus Christ, Rajiv, what the hell kind of place is this?" Paul asked. "This is supposed to be a business meeting."

"Shit, man, this is a whorehouse. I come here all the time to relax. I thought you might want to spend a little quality time here away from your diplomatic friends and maybe even get laid."

"That was very thoughtful of you, Rajiv, but no thanks. I'll finish my drink, and then I'm gone. Before I leave, I'll give you the time, date and place for our next meeting plus a couple of alternate times if one of us can't make the meeting. Don't be late. Even though this is Port of Spain, we'll work by Moscow rules. That means I'll wait three minutes past the scheduled time for a safe-house meeting and thirty seconds for a street meeting. We set our watches a half hour before the scheduled meeting by calling the local time telephone number."

Rajiv was Trinidadian, so he thought it was a great joke that he'd brought this CIA guy to a whorehouse for a clandestine meeting. He had a mind of his own, and Paul had to work all the time he knew Rajiv to keep him focused on their objectives. But he was sobered by Paul's instructions, and he proved to be reliable in making their meetings on time.

It was dark when Paul first met Rajiv, so he hadn't had an opportunity to see what he looked like. Now that they were together in daylight, he saw before him a thickset man of mixed Indian and black origin, common in Trinidad. He had a two- or three-day growth of beard and was dressed in a bush jacket (Paul never saw him when he wasn't wearing it, and he never saw it entirely clean), a wrinkled, stained pair of pants and sandals.

Rajiv worked hard at being non-conformist, but he was a great source in that place at that time. Paul never doubted for a moment that his motivation was money—he was well paid—but he proved to be worth it. Some of his information was checkable, particularly when he was reporting on Trinidad and Tobago government decisions.

Paul had access to a middle-level government official, and through him he found that Rajiv was reporting reliably. So Paul had a crosscheck on what Rajiv told him, and it turned out that Rajiv was telling him the truth and was frequently telling him more than anyone else was telling him. Langley was happy with him and so was Paul.

As time went on, and what was happening in the Caribbean became more important to CIA, Langley wanted a bit more insurance that Rajiv was not fabricating just to keep the money coming. Langley proposed that he be given a polygraph, a lie detector test. Paul cabled back that he doubted Rajiv would agree, but he would make it as palatable as he could and see what happened. He explained to Rajiv that this was routine with sources who were furnishing valuable information, and the polygraph should not be considered a signal that Langley or Paul questioned his reporting. Much to his surprise, Rajiv readily agreed to take the test, which would be given in a Miami hotel room.

Paul remained in the room throughout the test. When Rajiv was asked about his sexual preferences, he departed from the normal yes-no response to explain—graphically—why he was nuts about sex, and how sometimes he could not decide between a clean boy and a dirty girl. The operator was flustered by all this, and he tried hard to get Rajiv back on track. But Rajiv knew he had the operator off balance, so he just kept on about his lurid sex life.

The operator asked Paul out to the adjoining room, where he said, "Jesus, I've never tested anybody like this guy. He's nuts. Is any of that bullshit about his sex life and clean boys true?"

"It could be," Paul replied, "but I doubt it. I think he's just trying to make a joke of this whole thing."

"Well," said the operator, "apart from that disgusting sex stuff, it looks like he's telling the truth. He's clean on whether he's working for anyone else or misleading you in his reporting."

So Rajiv passed the polygraph and everybody was happy. Since they could not be seen together in public in Port of Spain, Paul proposed they have dinner together to celebrate. He made a reservation at a good restaurant in north Miami Beach. When Paul came for Rajiv at his hotel, he was wearing his bush jacket and hadn't shaved. When they arrived at the restaurant, the maître d' took one look at Rajiv and said to Paul, "Sir, I cannot honor your reservation. Your guest is not wearing a jacket. That's a requirement here for dinner."

Paul looked at Rajiv and grinned. Rajiv grinned back.

"I understand," Paul said. "Would you have a jacket in the cloak room you can perhaps loan my friend so that he and I may enjoy our dinner here this evening?"

The maître d' sniffed and glared at Paul. "Yes, of course," he said, "this doesn't happen often here, but we keep a small supply of jackets for those who are not appropriately dressed. Let me have a look."

He came back with a sport coat made for a 300-pound man; it was at least three sizes too big for Rajiv, but it did go on over the bush jacket. The sleeves came down to his fingernails.

"Shit, man," he said to Paul, checking the sleeves, "I look like I'm playing carnival. I'm hungry, but I'm not sure I want my dinner in this place."

"Rajiv, it's been a good day," Paul replied. "Let us not permit this asshole to spoil it for us. What we need is a couple of drinks and a steak, the best they've got. Okay?"

"Okay," said Rajiv, as they fell into step with the waiter showing them to their table. "It's your party."

Rajiv rolled his sleeves up to the wrist, and neither one said another word about how humiliating it must have been for Rajiv to sit there in a sport coat made for a 300-pound gorilla.

Back once again in the safe apartment in Port of Spain, Rajiv said, "Man, I sure learned a lot on this trip. I've been to Miami before—many times—but never like this. I'm black and there's not a damn thing I can do about it. Up in Miami, people looked at me like I just escaped from the zoo. I kept lookin' for black faces, so I could feel at home. But I only saw a few. Here at home, all the faces are black, and I don't even think about my blackness. I used to think about goin' up to the States to live and work. But no more. That ain't for me. It's for those folks standin' in long lines outside your consulate. I'm gonna have to stay here and do my little work thing, and keep messin' around with the whores and the rum and the steel bands. I'm stuck with that."

"Yeah, Rajiv, I guess you are. But if you change your mind and want to come up, and you need help with a green card or anything else, I'll be there for you."

"Thanks."

I should make clear that I knew nothing about Paul's sources, in Trinidad or anywhere else, while he was working with them. I learned of them many years after he retired and I interviewed him, just as I did for most of what I've written.

Paul's business in the Caribbean required occasional travel to Miami. The airline with the most convenient schedule was British West Indies Airlines (BWIA), owned and operated by the government of Trinidad and Tobago.

Trinidad has some of the most attractive females I have ever seen. Be they black, white, Chinese, East Indian or a mix—and most are a mix—they seem to be uniformly beautiful in face and form. BWIA had carefully selected the best looking of these girls for their flight attendants. While we were in Trinidad, ladies' skirts became shorter every day. The BWIA girls wore them shorter than anyone else.

On a flight one day to Miami, Paul was in an aisle seat. The flight attendant, a café-au-lait-complexioned girl of exceptional beauty, was serving a drink to the passenger in the window seat across the aisle. This required a lot of bending over. Paul found the girl's silk panties only inches from his face.

Never one to pass up an opportunity, Paul did not let his gaze wander. As he stared, he saw embroidered on one side of the panties the word "Fly." On the other cheek was "BWIA." Paul says he can't remember anything more Trinidadian than that.

Trinidad is famous for its carnival. It begins very early on the Monday morning preceding Ash Wednesday and continues until midnight on Tuesday. It was not uncommon for us to have thirty-five or forty for *j'ouvert* breakfast as carnival began.

There is a great deal of happy jumping around packed into those two days, and quite a let-down when it's all over. The celebrants are organized in bands of 200 or so, and their costumes express a theme. The steel bands are everywhere, playing music that invites, demands that the people in the streets dance to it.

Paul "played carnival" every year we lived in Port of Spain. He was happy to be a spear carrier, moving through the streets of Port of Spain, dancing to the outrageous music of the steel bands. When Yvonne heard the music, she would dance in the driveway with the supple, fluid movement only the Islanders have.

Our last year in Trinidad, Paul and a few others hired a small black boy, dressed him in a toreador costume and had him push a small cart right behind them filled with ice-cold rum punch, scotch, bourbon, gin, vodka, whatever. It didn't take long for their friends to find out what was in the cart, and they came home with a lot of empty bottles. Paul carried a large, white enameled cup that the little boy never allowed to go dry.

The route through the Port of Spain streets is over five miles long—I measured it myself in my car. Then the celebrants pass over a stage on the Savannah, a large, open rectangular park in the center of the city, where they expect to be greeted with shouts and applause. When the group Paul was with came across, I was sitting in the stands with Trinidadian friends. The small boy had his cup, and Paul had his arms around two beautiful Trinidadian girls. One of my friends turned to me and said, "Florence, don't you think he's kind of overdoing this business about getting to know the locals?"

We both made an effort—a happy one—to get to know the Trinidadians. We found them hedonistic, madcap and rarely responsible; but they are also generous, kind, hospitable, witty and articulate. We number many of them—black, white, and some in between—our good friends today.

So it would not be fair to say that our time in Trinidad was a total waste. But it was very close to that for Paul as a professional, committed to operations against the Soviets. As our time there drew to a close, he continued to probe for clues to explain his exile. He met with little success. He did, however, pick up vibrations now and again among friends and associates that he was in some kind of serious trouble.

•

Just before we left Trinidad, Paul had a visitor, an old friend who was a senior officer of the Western Hemisphere Division, responsible for the Port of Spain station. We had a pleasant dinner together, and then I left them because it was obvious they wanted to discuss business. Paul and the visitor took their cognac into the study, and I could hear the volume go up on the hi-fi as it blared the latest calypso tunes.

They had a few more cognacs before they got around to talking about how odd it was that Paul was here in Port of Spain. Finally, the visitor asked, "But don't you know why you went to the Farm and then came down here?"

"No, I don't. I've been trying to find out for seven years."

"Well, it's real simple. Jim Angleton has turned the Clandestine Service upside down looking for a KGB mole. The SR Division is paralyzed, dead in the water. It's like a graveyard. You're one of Jim's top suspects."

Paul was horrified. "But that's crazy. There can't be any evidence for that, and I ought to know. How did all this absurd stuff get started?"

"I honestly don't know. I've already told you more than I should have."

"But if those crazy bastards think I'm a traitor, why don't they face me with the charge, sweat me, polygraph me, arrest me? Why are they just letting me twist in the wind out here?"

"Whoa, boy, hold it. I'm not supposed to be talking to you about *any* of this. There's a conspiracy of silence in the Clandestine Service about your case. *Nobody* talks about it. And that's all I know anyway."

Paul was appalled at what he'd heard. But, always the optimist, he was confident he could track back into the Service and find the answers he sought. He was dead wrong—because he underestimated the strength and resilience of the conspiracy. Not for another five years—and then only under the strongest pressure he could bring to bear—was the Agency to admit there was a security charge against him in its records.

11. Stockholm Revisited

W HEN PAUL finished his tour in Trinidad, it had
been more than eight years since he returned to
Langley from Moscow and began a long downhill
slide. Without speaking to Tom K. or anyone else, he made an
appointment with the Inspector General on his first day back in
headquarters. This may not be considered such a serious step in
today's CIA—to air a grievance or blow the whistle on management—but Paul thought of it then as a grave move indeed. He
knew full well that Tom K. would not view his chat with the IG as
a positive development for the Service.

But Paul was weary of shadow boxing with Tom and the others. He wanted the cards out on the table where he could see them
and play a few of his own. He wanted to face his accusers. As the
best-informed person in this particular matter, he knew there
could be no truth in the accusation that he had spied for the KGB.
It simply never happened. He knew that and he wanted everyone
else to know that.

It turned out that he was to deal with the IG himself, Bill
Broe. Bill had been the chief of the Western Hemisphere Division
when Paul had been exiled to Trinidad. Hence, Bill was very much
aware of Paul's having become a "security problem." He knew all
about it and he knew that Paul knew he knew all about it.

They nonetheless observed the niceties and played out the cha-
rade. Bill listened patiently while Paul sketched out what had hap-

pened over the past eight years and told Bill of his deep concern that an alleged security problem might underlie these strange events. A point Paul wanted to make with Bill was that he had become a senior officer of the Clandestine Service at age forty-five. Given normal circumstances, he could have looked forward to fifteen or more years of increasing responsibility and challenge—and advancement—in the Service. Instead, he had spent the last eight years going backwards, the victim of a phantom charge with never an opportunity to defend himself. Paul said he wanted to know why he had never been officially informed of the charge, and he wanted Bill to tell him what could be done to correct the situation.

Bill heard Paul out, asked a few questions he already knew the answers to, and agreed to get back to Paul promptly. He called a few days later, and asked that Paul come to see him. He said he had discussed the case with Tom K., who agreed to write a memorandum for the record. (The memo was classified, so I never saw it until Paul obtained a "sanitized" copy through a Freedom of Information request.) The memo makes no mention of any security charge or any security-related difficulty. Tom repeats the same tired rationalizations he offered Paul for the assignments to training and the Caribbean. He adds that he would not want to see Paul's having served in these assignments "in the interest of the Service" "lost in the records." In Paul's view, this was a unique document in that it represents a strong recommendation for promotion from the chief of the Service "at the next convening of the appropriate board."

But Paul had been on the shelf for almost nine years. The few promotions to be had on that level were going—Paul thought correctly—to candidates who did not have an unexplained nine-year hiatus in their career patterns. Tom K. must have known that the only certain way for Paul to be promoted was for him to plead Paul's case with Richard Helms, then serving his final year as Director of Central Intelligence.

Tom K. chose not to speak with Helms about a promotion for Paul. Paul didn't know why, but thought perhaps Tom's going to Helms in Paul's behalf would be perceived as Tom's accepting responsibility for the shabby treatment Paul had received.

There was another likely reason for Helms' not taking an initiative in Paul's case. Helms was known to be the consummate bureaucrat, a survivor, the best in the Agency. Catching Helms off base in *anything* was just about impossible. Paul's case had been bungled from the start to finish. If Helms now moved to help Paul, it might be perceived that he played a role in the Keystone Kops scenario that brought Paul down. Helms was not about to be drawn into that kind of mess.

But he knew Paul well enough to know he was incapable of treason. That was the shame of it.

Tom K. did, however, arrange for Paul's partial rehabilitation. He saw to it that Paul was assigned to Stockholm as chief of station—his third and final station chief job. A lot of water had passed under the Stockholm bridges since our first assignment there seventeen years earlier. When we returned, we enjoyed renewing acquaintances with Swedish friends, some of whom we had corresponded with for more than fifteen years. And the station kept Paul fully engaged, so it proved a worthwhile tour for both of us.

We were fortunate to inherit housing from Paul's predecessor this time around in Stockholm, which we considered a blessing. The house was old, large and comfortable, situated on the island of Lidingö, only a few miles from the center of Stockholm. Paul's station and embassy responsibilities quickly persuaded us we were going to need a housekeeper who could cook, clean and serve.

We found the availability of domestics was nil, even worse than it had been when we arrived in Stockholm seventeen years earlier. There was simply nothing available. I did some research, and we decided to place an ad in a Madrid newspaper and one in Edinburgh, Scotland. We chose Spain and Scotland because those countries had the highest rate of unemployment in Europe.

About a week after our ad appeared in Edinburgh, I had a well-written letter, together with a résumé, from an applicant. The résumé, as I recall, cited employment as a chef in hotels, country clubs and on a cruise ship. David had also worked as a housekeeper for an invalid couple. He sounded right for us. After an exchange of letters, I sent him an airline ticket. Paul picked him up at the airport and found he was wearing the tightest pair of slacks either of us had ever seen. We gave that no thought, assuming that was just the way things were in Scotland.

As David settled in, he proved to be as good as his résumé. He kept the house spotlessly clean, he was a gourmet cook, he served professionally, his manners reflected a good upbringing, his attitude was positive, and we were very happy with him. Paul checked him out routinely with Langley and London Station. There were no traces.

Soon, however, we learned something about David for which we were unprepared. We had several attractive young secretaries in the embassy, and I'd heard they were spending a lot of time at home, reading and watching television. David was a pleasant, good-looking man, and I told him I would be happy to arrange an introduction to one or all, and he might want to date one of these girls. David didn't say no, but he certainly didn't jump on my offer.

After I tried this a few times, he said, "Mrs. G., you've got to understand. I'm not interested in women. I'm interested in men."

This came as a surprise to me, but I didn't want to appear shocked. So I closed it out by saying, "Okay, David, I understand. But you've got to arrange that on your own."

I talked to Paul, knowing he would be concerned about the potential for scandal. He said, "David's been good to us, and I like him very much, but we may have to let him go if his lifestyle begins to give us problems. That kind of thing gets around very fast. The Swedes are much more tolerant of homosexuality than we are, but the people I talk to may begin to wonder about the security consequences of something like this. I know David's okay, I'm not worried about that. But let's keep an eye out for trouble."

Paul was right about the word getting around quickly. A few months after David began to work for us, large British and American luxury cars (and an occasional scattering of Volvos) began appearing in the driveway (one at a time) below David's garage apartment. He explained that these were friends he'd met in gay bars around the city. He said I needn't worry.

"These guys are not criminals, they come from the best families in town, they're the local gentry."

But I did worry, and I went back to Paul with my concerns. I was surprised to hear him say, "Florence, David's an adult, and we shouldn't intrude on his personal life. He's not a problem now. If he becomes one, we'll have to let him go."

David never became a problem. In fact, he proved even more a friend than we expected. He was a strong man, and when Paul would jog in the dark, early-morning hours and the demonstrators were at our gates (see below), David offered to go with him because he "needed the exercise." Paul thanked him but made it clear it wasn't necessary.

When we left Sweden, we arranged for David to go to work for another embassy family. I mentioned David's homosexuality, and they said that did not concern them. For a while we corresponded with David. In the beginning, he would write once a month to tell me how he was getting on. That lapsed to once every three to six months. Until two years ago, we heard from him every Christmas, and his card would be filled with news. Since then, nothing. I heard from my Swedish lady in the embassy that David had gone to live with a Lutheran priest. I still think of him often, and worry about him, especially in light of the AIDS epidemic.

The Stockholm archipelago spans more than 22,000 islands. So it is understandable that the Stockholmers have a love affair with boats. Those who can afford it—and in many cases, those who can't—own a boat, everything from a sailing dinghy to sixty- and seventy-foot motor sailers. They spend every summer week-end in the archipelago, overnighting tied up to a favorite island. Those who own the larger boats spend their summer vacations (frequently a month or two) on their boats, venturing out into the Baltic and up and down the east and west coasts of Sweden.

A good deal depends upon the summer weather, always unpre-dictable. If the Swedes have a summer filled with sunshine, they charge their batteries and they're much better prepared to cope with the long, dark winter. Given a summer filled with clouds and rain— it happens often—and the Swedes become bears in the winter.

We elected not to own our own boat during our first tour in Sweden, because it was less trouble and less expensive to sail with our Swedish friends. They introduced us to the archipelago, and we found the blue water and the untouched landscape of the rocky, primitive islands what we needed for restful weekends. The Swedes have been taught from childhood that they are restored and refreshed by communing with nature. Paul and I were surprised to find that it worked. We watched it work for the Swedes, and we found that it worked for us, but maybe not as well as it did for them.

During our first tour in Sweden, Paul went a bit too far in trying to fall in with the Swedes and their fascination with boating. He had a Swedish friend, Sven, who owned a large sailboat, maybe a fifty-footer. Sven entered his boat in a demanding sailing race called the *Gotland Runt.* The contest started from the yacht club at Sandhamn, close to where the archipelago gives out onto the Baltic, then across the Baltic to the island of Gotland, around Gotland, and back to Sandhamn. Given a fair wind, a good sailor could cover the route in something like seventy-two hours.

After he entered his boat, Sven started looking around for a crew. He recruited Paul, who thought he was going for a joyride, and a Belgian and a Frenchman, both experienced sailors. Everybody got a nice send-off from Sandhamn, and they entered the Baltic at about dusk. Paul had never been in the Baltic in a sailboat, and he found the Baltic is a very choppy sea. He quickly became worthless as a crew member, and began asking Sven and the others how far it was to Gotland. Paul told me when he got home that, if Sven hadn't stopped long enough to let him off at Gotland, he was going to jump off the boat and swim ashore. As it turned out, Sven lost interest in the race and decided to spend a couple of pleasant days on the island. All of his crew thought this was a master stroke, and they sailed home a couple of days later in brilliant sunshine.

We looked around carefully before we bought our own boat at the beginning of our second tour in Stockholm. We finally settled on an Albin 25, a fine weekend boat. It's broad in the beam, and that makes for comfortable accommodations. It sleeps four, and that was just right for our needs. It's not built for speed, far from it, but it was comfortable and reliable, and that suited us fine. In any case, I never saw a water skier in the archipelago.

I ordered our boat in red, white and blue, and decorated the interior to match. When we placed our order, the factory manager expressed astonishment and then rage that we wanted to change the standard colors, but he reluctantly agreed to fix everything as we wanted. Wherever we appeared in the archipelago, the Swedes would cry, "Here come the Americans."

Paul bought lots of charts and felt his way around the maze of islands cautiously. Then one weekend we were invited to a dance at the Sandhamn Yacht Club, not far from the entrance to the Baltic Sea. We made it down there with only a few detours. Paul had taken a course and passed the test, in Swedish, for an amateur marine license. So Paul learned something about navigation in the archipelago, and that helped us make it to Sandhamn without getting too badly lost.

We met Swedes at Sandhamn we would not have had the opportunity to know in Stockholm. They were part of a boat culture that kept them sailing the archipelago eight or nine months of the year. One older couple told us a story about a Stockholm banker that became part of Swedish boating lore.

The banker owned a large, luxurious sailing yacht that carried a crew of three or four. The helmsman was a Norwegian named Pettersen. The banker liked to handle the sails himself. One evening around tea time, Pettersen brought the yacht into the Sandhamn docking area. The banker had made it clear to Pettersen that they were going to make the landing on the sails, no motor. Most of the people tied up at Sandhamn were out on the stern of their boats having tea or something a lot stronger. That meant that the banker would have a large audience for the feat of nautical dexterity he planned. That suited him down to the ground. He unfortunately left the mainsail up a few seconds too long. A puff of wind caught it, and he realized they were not going to be able to make a neat turn into the wind to stop the boat before they smashed into the dock.

Showing remarkable presence of mind, the banker turned and shouted, "Pettersen, hit something cheap."

•

Perhaps three months after we arrived in Stockholm, we attended a reception at the Soviet Embassy. The hosts showed a boring documentary film in a small, sparsely furnished theater. The Swedes had introduced fuel rationing and the Soviets, in their eagerness to comply, had overdone it. It was like sitting inside a freezer. Even the men, dressed in wool suits, were uncomfortable. Paul kept blowing on his hands and finally resorted to keeping them in his pockets.

When the film concluded, we all trooped out, wanting a drink or anything else that would warm us. A line formed at the bar. While we were standing there, a neatly dressed man of medium height and strong-looking build came up to Paul and held out his hand.

"I am Viktor Maksimovich Fedorov [not his real name] of this embassy, and you are Paul Garbler of the American Embassy." His English was excellent.

"Yes, I'm Paul Garbler," Paul replied. "How did you know?"

"From a picture I received a few weeks ago. It was taken in Moscow, when you were there as CIA station chief. In the picture you are wearing a very nice mink hat. Did you bring it to Stockholm?"

"As a matter of fact, I did. Who sent you the picture of me in the nice mink hat?"

"Friends in Moscow. You see, I am stationed here now, and my friends wanted me to know that you too are working here now."

"That was good of them. I wish my people at home were that good to me. I don't have a photo of you in a nice mink hat." Paul turned as if to terminate the conversation and get his drink, but he didn't know Fedorov.

"Mr. Garbler," he said, "in my country those who work hard for the state, like you and I do, don't stand in lines. That's the way it is in this embassy, and I don't want you to stand in line here."

He turned, spied a waiter with a loaded tray, and snapped his fingers. The waiter responded with alacrity. Fedorov selected three oversized shot glasses filled with straight vodka and handed two to Paul and me, keeping the fullest one for himself.

"Mr. Garbler," he said, "I'm sure you speak Russian, and maybe your wife does too, maybe better than you. So you both will understand my toast."

He raised his glass and said, "*Na zdorovye*—to your health." He then tossed back all of the vodka and smiled his satisfaction. Paul followed suit. I swallowed half of mine and felt tears start in my eyes.

I heard Fedorov's appreciative chuckle. "Very good, Mrs. Garbler, that's excellent. I can see you've been helping your husband in his work. I wish my wife was so cooperative."

When I felt it safe to speak, I asked, "Is your wife here this evening, Mr. Fedorov?"

"No. She has a cold and didn't want to stand around in our refrigerated embassy. This is crazy."

"I'm sorry she's not well. I hope it won't be for long."

Fedorov looked at me from under lowered lids for just a moment, as if to question my interest and wonder if I was trying to say that I didn't really believe his wife had a cold.

It was obvious to me that Paul didn't want to spend the evening chit-chatting with Fedorov. So I said, "We really must be going," which I knew was exactly what Paul wanted me to say.

Fedorov let his gaze wander around the reception hall, where people were forming up into conversation islands and said, "I'm neglecting our guests. The ambassador will be displeased. But I want you to know that I enjoyed meeting both of you. I hope to see more of you. *Do svidanye*—until we meet again."

We saw Fedorov now and then at social events, never with his wife. We saw him once at the Palace, which surprised us. It was obvious that he knew his way around and had little, if any, concern about mixing with foreigners, as did so many of his countrymen we had come to know over the years.

Paul reported the contact to Langley, adding that he assumed Fedorov was KGB and intended to ask him and his wife to dinner at our home. (Paul asked for traces and learned that Fedorov was confirmed KGB.) Soviet officials do not customarily accept such invitations, but Paul wanted to see how different Fedorov *really* was.

When Paul called and extended the invitation, Fedorov begged off, saying that his wife was in Moscow visiting their young son, and he preferred to wait until she returned. Paul offered lunch instead, and he accepted. He and Paul had a pleasant lunch out on our patio. About a month later, he asked us to dinner. We thought we were going to his apartment and would finally meet the phantom Mrs. Fedorov. Instead, we dined with Fedorov alone on one of the Soviet cruise vessels that visited Stockholm regularly.

It was an excellent meal, and we congratulated Fedorov on his choice of restaurant, but added we were a little disappointed that we had not gone to his home, where we might have met his wife. Fedorov beamed at our praise and said something about his wife not being as good a cook as the chef on the ship.

When dinner was over, and we were having coffee and liqueurs in the ship's lounge (there were no passengers in sight, so we assumed Fedorov had booked the entire vessel for the evening), Fedorov said, "Paul, I know you play golf, and I'm told you are pretty good at it."

"I see you've been gathering biographic information on me, Viktor. But your sources are not reliable. It's true that I play golf, but it's not true that I'm good at it. Better recruit some new sources, Viktor."

"You're probably being overly modest, Paul. The reason I'm interested in golf is that I have heard from some of my comrades in Moscow that our government has agreed to build a golf course not far from the city. I want to be one of the first to play there. For that, I need your help in selecting equipment, and I would like you to teach me the fundamentals. Do you think you could do that for me?"

Paul was surprised to hear about the new golf course. He had always believed that the Soviets had built a nine-hole course for President Eisenhower when he was scheduled to visit in 1960. When we were stationed in Moscow, Paul had asked his Soviet contacts about it frequently. But the Soviets treated it as classified, probably because Gary Powers's U-2 was shot down in May 1960, an event which led to the cancellation of Eisenhower's visit. Now here was Fedorov talking about a new course.

We knew Fedorov was something of a social climber, and we could guess how important it would be to him to be one of the first Russians to own golf clubs and play the game.

So Paul said, "Viktor, I will be happy to take you out to my club and advise you on which golf clubs to buy. You can buy them on my account and then repay me. But I can't teach you the game because I'm not good enough to do that. First I have to teach myself. But I will introduce you to the club professional, and I'm sure he will be happy to give you lessons. How's that?"

"That's very kind of you, and I'll call next week to arrange our visit to your club. We don't have country clubs in Russia, and I'm curious to see what yours is like."

So Fedorov and Paul went out to the club and Fedorov bought clubs, a golf bag and a pair of golf shoes. He was as happy as a child at Christmas with his purchases. It seemed to Paul that even if he never used the equipment, he expected to make points with his Moscow "friends" just *showing* it to them.

About six months later, Sam Snead came to Stockholm to play an exhibition match with "Tumba" Johansson at our club. Tumba was a large, very strong young man who had been a star on the Swedish national hockey team. When he stopped playing hockey, he took up golf. He was Sweden's best. He could hit the ball out of sight, but he never knew where it was going to come down.

Paul asked Fedorov to be our guest for the exhibition. He readily agreed. We were surprised at how little he knew. At the first tee, his question was, "Why are they putting the ball on top of that peg? Why is he using a wood club instead of a metal one?"

So we knew that Fedorov had not followed up on Paul's suggestion that he take instruction from the pro. But we patiently answered all his questions, and he was obviously delighted to be a spectator.

Paul tried to explain some of the fine points. On the first nine, Snead had driven in the fairway but there was a thick stand of trees between his ball and the green. "You see, Viktor, that is a difficult shot for Sam. To begin with, he can't see the flag. And he must hit the ball high enough to clear the trees and far enough to reach the green. Not an easy shot."

"But he is a professional," Fedorov replied, "he'll make it okay, just watch."

Snead hit a perfect shot to within three feet of the flag. Fedorov turned to Paul and said, "See? I told you, he's a professional."

Paul said nothing. What could he say?

A few holes later, Snead hit over the green and had a tricky chip shot coming back. The green sloped sharply away from where his ball lay, and it looked almost impossible to stop the ball near the hole. Paul said, "Okay, Viktor, this is really a tough shot for Sam. Once the ball hits the green, it will probably run clear to the opposite side. Sam's a good chipper, but this is very difficult." Fedorov said, "Paul, don't worry. Snead is a professional, he knows how to stop the ball near the hole."

Snead chipped in. Everyone clapped, but Fedorov did not. Once again, he turned to Paul with a knowing smile and said, "I knew he could do it. That's why he's a professional."

So it went for eighteen holes. It seemed that Fedorov had learned more about golf in a few hours than Paul had in ten years. When we walked him back to his car, Fedorov said with a broad smile, "Paul, maybe you were right about not teaching me golf. I need someone who knows a lot more about the game." Then he drove off, leaving us standing in a large cloud of dust.

"Florence," Paul said in a choked voice, "most of the Russians I've known are overbearing. But this is one overbearing son-ofabitch like I've never met before."

In April 1975, seven terrorists of the West German Baader-Meinhof Gang shot their way into the West German Embassy in Stockholm and seized a dozen hostages, including the German ambassador.

The takeover began at noon and lasted until about midnight. The terrorists mortally wounded the German military attaché, and later they shot the commercial attaché and hurled his body out onto the street from a third-story window. The commercial attaché lunched frequently in the cafeteria in the American Embassy, and Paul knew him as a kind, gentle, soft-spoken man. What those thugs did to him seemed to all of us a mindless atrocity.

The terrorists demanded the release of twenty-six comrades held in West German jails. If they were not released as they asked, they threatened to kill the hostages one by one and blow up the embassy.

On the top floor of the embassy, the terrorists wired together a large quantity of TNT while they held the hostages on a lower floor. One of the terrorists working with the explosives accidently tripped one of the wires and set off a massive explosion.

The rear of the American Embassy was less than ten feet from one side of the German Embassy. Paul, sitting in his darkened office for most of the night, had a birds-eye view of what was happening around the German Embassy. He called in the station communicator, and they sent situation reports as events unfolded. About midnight, Paul saw a brilliant flash and heard a loud *whump* as he watched the roof of the German Embassy rise about three feet and fall back in pieces. The entire top floor quickly caught fire and Swedish firefighters rushed in as the confused terrorists, caught off guard by the premature explosion, stumbled out of the building.

A gun battle with the police ensued, and six of the terrorists were captured while one, a woman, shot it out with the police in the burning embassy, where she had chosen to make a stand.

A few years earlier, Paul attended a meeting in Curacao called by Egil "Bud" Krogh, then President Nixon's anti-drug coordinator in the White House. Krogh, a fine young man, was later caught up in the Watergate scandal because he served as head of the "plumbers," the squad that was supposed to plug the leaks for Nixon. He was sentenced to two to six years in prison, where he spent six months.

In any case, Paul spoke with Krogh at the Curacao meeting, citing his concerns about international terrorism, some of it sponsored and sheltered by the Soviet Union. With leaders like Muammar Gaddafi, Hafez al-Assad and Yasser Arafat, determined to achieve their objectives through relatively inexpensive and difficult-to-combat terrorism, Paul believed it was one of the most serious threats to world peace in the 1970-80s. Krogh thought it might be a good idea to have a counter-terrorism referent in the

Nixon White House, who would function very much as he did in the war against drugs. It was one thing to discuss terrorism in a vacuum. It was another for Paul to witness terrorism up close, first hand, to realize how evil it really was.

Our second tour in Stockholm was marred by an exceedingly unpleasant happening. A former CIA officer/renegade named Philip Agee came to Stockholm near the end of our time there and identified for the leftist press Paul and every member of the Stockholm station. He had done this in several European capitals on his way to Stockholm, but that did not soften the blow for Paul. It turned his stomach to have the men and women in his station and their families suffer exposure at the hands of a turncoat like Agee.

When Agee came to town, Stockholm's leftists organized protest rallies outside our home. The police were there in force to see that no one crossed the line onto our property. The demonstrators shouted obscenities and threw eggs and tomatoes at our gateposts. Caught in the frenzy of their shouting and fist-shaking, the Swedes still remained non-violent. So we could come and go as we wished. But it was a sickening experience for Paul, who had always lived his cover, to have his name in the Stockholm dailies and to suffer the hoots and catcalls of the demonstrators.

We returned from Stockholm to Langley during the summer of 1976. As is routine for officers returning from abroad, Paul was given a thorough physical exam. The Agency doctor found a lump on one lobe of his thyroid. A specialist was called in. He confirmed the growth and recommended that it be removed surgically at once. The doctor was the head of the Vince Lombardi clinic at Georgetown University Hospital, so we were not going to argue with his advice. Paul had surgery. The growth was found to be malignant. The surgeon had removed only one lobe of the gland, and now he wanted to repeat the surgery and get the second lobe, just in case it, too, was infected.

We discussed the second surgery at length with the surgeon. Paul told him there had been an unusually high incidence of cancer of all kinds at the Moscow embassy while we were there. Some of our friends had died of the disease. The government knew that the Soviets were directing a mysterious low-frequency "ray" at the embassy at that time, and there was speculation that the ray had caused the cancer. The surgeon thought that possible and, sensing our uncertainty about another surgery, suggested that we get a second opinion. So we went up to New York to see a head and neck specialist from the Sloan-Kettering Memorial Institute. He examined Paul and told us we could have the second lobe removed if we wanted or we could leave it alone. We thanked him and taxied directly to the Oyster Bar in the Plaza Hotel, where we had several drinks and dozens of oysters and clams. I knew Paul didn't want the second operation, but I had remained neutral up to then. After my second vodka on the rocks, I told my friend I really didn't want him to have the second surgery. Celebrating, we shook on that.

The Agency took care of all the bills for Paul's treatment at Georgetown University Hospital, in Innsbruck and in Wiesbaden and Bethesda. Paul couldn't figure out how the professor in Innsbruck was paid, but we never heard anything about any of those bills. I'm sure that was part of how the Agency takes care of its own.

Tom K. retired while we were in Stockholm, and Paul heard nothing from him or anyone else about the alleged security problem. Hearing nothing, Paul made up his mind he would make one last attempt to clear his name.

As soon as he was well enough to return to work after thyroid surgery, Paul addressed the Inspector General once again, this time in writing. He referred to his earlier request for an investigation and asked that the case be reopened. If no other purpose was to be served, he wished to have his name cleared of any security charge, something Tom K. had never been willing to admit existed. Paul's memo was dated December 8, 1976. He had returned from Moscow in July 1964. That's more than *twelve* years.

Paul did not hear from the IG for several months. When he did, he was advised that a report of the investigation had been sent to the Acting Deputy Director of Central Intelligence, John F. Blake. A few days later, Paul received a memo from Jack Blake.

This was the first time in more than twelve years that CIA admitted there was a security charge against Paul. Jack Blake, speaking for the Agency, acknowledged the charge and, in the same breath declared it invalid. He wrote that "the previously raised security issue has been fully resolved in your favor." It is also worth noting that Jack Blake regretted "the adverse effect the now-resolved security questions have had on your career."

Paul knew Jack Blake well enough to be certain that he was a gentleman of high integrity. There was consequently no question in his mind that Jack meant sincerely every word he had written. Which left Paul with a problem: was the apology for having needlessly given him and his family so many years of grief enough to countervail what had been done to us?

Paul and I spent hours discussing everything that had happened to us since our return from Moscow in 1964. He took my views into account—I was content to settle for the apology—in arriving at his own decision that the Agency's apology, well-intentioned as it was, could not possibly redress the wrong that had been done us. Paul said he was reminded of the rapist who, when he has finished his business and is zipping up his fly, tells the hapless victim, still on the ground, how sorry he is for his reprehensible behavior.

In late November 1977 (it took Paul several months to reach a decision) Paul wrote to Director Stansfield Turner, asking that he approve "compensation for the financial disadvantage and emotional stress my family and I have suffered since circa mid-1964 as a consequence of a groundless security charge...."

Director Turner replied on December, 28, 1977, three days before Paul retired. Paul obtained an unclassified copy of this memorandum through an FOIA request and showed it to me. Turner wrote: "I am unable to make you whole for any harm to your career which may have resulted from the charge." Further, "I believe there is no way for you to be compensated other than through a private bill in Congress." Still further, "I wish sincerely that there were some effective action I could take to undo this wrong."

Paul was resolved that he would run the string out as far as he could. He told me he would take his case to the Senate Select

Committee on Intelligence, the Intelligence Oversight Board (if they would be willing to hear him out), and even into the White House, if he could find someone there who would listen. He quickly discovered that the way to reach the people who should review his case was through the use of an attorney. Immediately after retirement, Paul met with an attorney in one of Washington's most respected law firms. The attorney's judgment was that the case had merit, and he agreed to take it on for a much reduced fee.

During his first meeting with the attorney, Paul made it clear that his ultimate objective was not money. He explained that he had met with Jack Blake and the Inspector General the week before his retirement. He told them he was not really seeking money, and both had professed they understood. All Paul wanted was some kind of good faith gesture from CIA that would say, "All right, the institution made a mistake. Now we want to do something for you that will prove you could not have been guilty as charged."

Paul's only recourse, as the attorney saw it, was to seek compensation through a private bill. In pursuit of a private bill, Paul's attorney touched base with the appropriate checkpoints in Congress and the Executive Branch. He found it to be the unanimous view that, for a private bill to be successful, CIA support was essential.

"That's no problem," Paul told the attorney. "Turner has written he wants to help any way he can."

So the attorney wrote and asked for CIA's support in putting before the Congress a request for a private bill. CIA's General Counsel, Tony Lapham, replied that *CIA could not support a private bill but would not oppose it.*

Laying Turner's letter alongside Lapham's, the attorney was astonished at the duplicity, and said, "Let's go talk to the Senate Select Committee on Intelligence."

They did, and they got a fair hearing and all the cooperation they could have hoped for. In the end, it was the SSCI that found a way for the Agency to compensate Paul as he had requested.

12. How Did It Happen?

IN OCTOBER 1949, Harold Adrian Russell "Kim" Philby arrived in Washington. He was a member of the British Establishment, a highly regarded MI-6 (British Intelligence) officer, and he was frequently mentioned as a possible future chief of MI-6. He was also the most capable, productive spy ever fielded by the KGB, which he served faithfully and well for more than three decades.

In Washington, Philby's job was to liaise with the CIA and FBI. His principal contact in CIA was James Angleton. He and Angleton lunched together frequently. Philby's capacity for alcohol was legend in the British Service; Angleton enjoyed a like reputation in the CIA. There is a routine requirement for a "contact" report every time a CIA official meets with a representative of a foreign government (i.e., topics discussed, what did you say, what did he say, etc.). After Angleton left CIA, a search was made of his files for contact reports covering the long, boozy luncheon meetings with Philby. None was ever found.

As time passed, there were some in CIA who believed Philby was working for the Russians. Not Angleton, he was Philby's staunchest defender. Imagine how humiliating it must have been for Angleton when Philby, finally accepting that the game was over, fled to Moscow from Lebanon in 1963. Later, in 1969, Philby rubbed salt in Angleton's wounds when he wrote in his book, *My Silent War,* of how he had duped Angleton.

After giving me the background on Philby, Paul said, "Now let's shift gears and focus on the KGB Center in Moscow. Sitting there, reading Philby's reporting on Angleton is an alert, bright, ambitious KGB officer. He wants to make a big score. He begins to realize that one of the most powerful men in CIA (Angleton) is a very strange fellow indeed. He is intimately familiar with Angleton's drinking habits, foibles and eccentricities. He knows that it is Angleton's job to defend against penetrations of the CIA and he knows from Philby that Angleton fears that the KGB has already made such a penetration, very much as it penetrated MI-6.

"So he looks around for a soulmate for Angleton, someone who will be able to fuel Angleton's suspicions and feed his paranoia. He knows he will not be permitted to use a highly valuable officer to send to Angleton, never to return to the KGB. So he settles on Major Anatoliy Golitsyn, who has never done much for the KGB. Then he has him posted to the Soviet embassy in Helsinki, which is much like sending him to Minsk. Helsinki in 1961 was a city owned by the Soviets and the KGB had free run.

"According to plan, Golitsyn requests asylum of the CIA station chief in Helsinki and is flown to the States. After his arrival in the U.S., Golitsyn is asked by the then Director of CIA, Allen Dulles, whether he knows of any penetrations of CIA. Golitsyn says no, the same answer he gave his Soviet Bloc Division debriefers, who do not hold him in high regard. But, from the Philby material, Golitsyn's KGB control knows that Angleton wants to hear that there is a mole. So when he talks to Angleton, Golitsyn says yes, there is a mole. He is not able to identify the mole precisely, but he has a few tantalizing tidbits, like his KGB code name is "Sasha," his last name begins with "K," and he served in Germany.

"If Angleton is foolish enough—he was—to give Golitsyn highly classified operational and personnel files, so that Golitsyn himself can put together the pieces of the jigsaw puzzle and nail the mole, the take from the KGB operation becomes incredible. The KGB has never had anything like it. They are looking at CIA's most carefully guarded secrets. And there is an unexpected dividend! If the KGB has a high-level mole sitting astride CIA's

Soviet operations, why should the CIA waste valuable time and money to pursue operations that are known to the KGB from their inception? The dividend cannot be believed at the KGB Center. With Golitsyn at his side, Angleton paralyzes CIA's Soviet operations for at least ten years. *Ten years.*

"Golitsyn's KGB control foresees the threat that would come from a *genuine* KGB defector. He would be able to debunk the mole story and other provocative material Golitsyn has been feeding Angleton. So Golitsyn is briefed to tell Angleton that the KGB would send out *false* defectors to discredit the truths he is telling Angleton. (There was an important KGB defector a few years after Golitsyn arrived in the U.S. Angleton immediately declared him a phoney.)"

Does Paul have any hard evidence to support the theory that the KGB sent Golitsyn to Angleton? No. But let's focus for a moment on some strange coincidences that emerged from the Angleton-Golitsyn relationship: It turned out that they were members of the same "flat earth" society, i.e., they both believed that the Sino-Soviet split was a fraud and deception aimed at confusing the West. Jim Angleton believed that until the day he died. Golitsyn wrote a book, *New Lies for Old*, in which he explains why he thinks this is so. Could it be only coincidence that Golitsyn and Angleton are both believers in a "flat earth"? Possible, but it seems unlikely. Philby had listened to Angleton—over cocktails, highballs, wine and cognac—propound the theory that the KGB had a sinister master plot to destroy America and the Western World. Was it a coincidence that Golitsyn confirmed the plot, and asked for $15 million to counter it? Possible, but hardly likely. Was it a coincidence that Golitsyn told Angleton that Averell Harriman, a respected diplomat and former American ambassador in Moscow, had been recruited by the KGB, when Angleton already had his doubts about Harriman? And that they agreed that Henry Kissinger would bear watching? These were not coincidences. Golitsyn knew what Angleton wanted to hear because his KGB control had told him how to sing Angleton's song, and he was feeding Angleton information he knew would excite him and build Angleton's confidence in him.

After he arrived in Moscow, Philby wrote in his book that he continued to work for the KGB. Is it not likely that, from 1963 on, he could have been coaching Golitsyn from the sidelines as Angleton dug himself an ever-deeper hole in his feverish search for the mole?

After poring over scores of personnel and operational files—only Angleton and his staff of mole hunters would know how many—Golitsyn selected Paul's "little man" (Igor Orlov) in Berlin as the mole. He may have had good reason for his choice—Paul doesn't know how it was done. It should be noted, however, that Orlov's alias in Berlin was (K)oischwitz. When Golitsyn was reminded that he had told Angleton and others that there was a "high level" mole, and Orlov was a lowly principal agent in charge of eleven hookers and a one-armed piano player in Berlin, Golitsyn reversed course at once and said, "But you don't understand. Of course Orlov was low level. But his job was to recruit his case officers to the KGB cause. He would try to do this with every one of his case officers. If one of his case officers did not report a recruitment attempt, that case officer had been recruited."

During the time Orlov worked for CIA, he may have had as many as a dozen case officers. One of these, Sam Wilson, went on to become an Army lieutenant general in charge of the Defense Intelligence Agency. Another, David Murphy, rose to become the chief of CIA's Soviet Bloc Division.

Did either one report a recruitment attempt by Orlov? Of course not. Did Orlov try to recruit Paul? Paul smiles at the notion and says, "He wouldn't dare." This was the kind of "evidence" Angleton and the mole hunters had against Paul. I would think a child would know better than to believe a story like that.

Paul does not understand why Angleton was so fascinated by Golitsyn. Insofar as he is concerned, Golitsyn was not fit to carry Jim Angleton's briefcase. He is totally convinced that Golitsyn was sent to Angleton, that Philby played an important role in the operation, and that the operation was successful beyond the KGB's wildest dreams.

This was a disgraceful time in the history of the Clandestine Service. Paul and many of his former associates believe that management, right up to and including Director Richard Helms, was as much responsible for the disgrace as Angleton was. The working level of the Clandestine Service knew that Angleton was a menace, a loose cannon, a man with authority but no responsibility. Director Helms permitted him the authority but did not hold him accountable for his bizarre and destructive behavior. Helms chose to ignore Angleton's machinations, and he allowed Angleton and his consort Golitsyn to rampage through the Clandestine Service, where they destroyed reputations and paralyzed operations.

While Angleton was playing out his fantasy about a mole, there were others, selfishly and ruthlessly ambitious, who fell into step with him in order to pursue their own agendas. So it wasn't all Angleton's fault, not by any means.

At last Paul knew who had destroyed him and why. When he finally learned the truth, he found it so absurd that he couldn't believe CIA's professional senior echelon had behaved so much like inept bunglers. It wasn't easy for him to accept that Angleton and Golitsyn had been allowed to play Russian roulette with his reputation and do grievous harm to him and his family.

We never discussed Paul's problem with Susan. It wasn't that we didn't trust her. On the contrary, we knew that if we told her what was happening, wild horses could not drag a single word from her about this sordid affair. But we felt it would not be fair to unload Paul's problem on her when there was nothing she could do to help.

Quite apart from what Susan and I experienced, consider for a moment how Paul felt when he began to read mistrust in the eyes of his associates and friends. When those with whom he worked turned over the papers on their desks when he entered the room. When a knot of officers chattering away in the corridor would quickly disperse when he approached. When a colleague and his wife turned their backs to us when Paul tried to introduce a friend at a cocktail party. When just about everyone he knew and trusted in the Service dealt with him warily, never uttering an extra word, frequently pausing in mid-sentence to be sure not to say too much.

After Paul retired, he joined the Association of Former Intelligence Officers (AFIO). A few months later, he attended an AFIO luncheon. Luncheon over, he was seated with a few friends, talking about old times. Tom Karamessines walked across the room and stopped at their table. Paul's friends rose to greet him and shake hands. Paul remained seated and tried to ignore him. Then Tom put out his hand, very close to Paul's face, not speaking. Paul stared at the hand for a long time. Then he rose and shook hands with Tom.

Tom said, "Paul, I came over to tell you, you did okay."

Paul started to say, "Maybe I did okay, Tom, but how about you? Did you do okay?" but thought better of it. He had made up his mind not to succumb to bitterness over his experience.

That was as close as Tom K. ever came to admitting that Paul's was a special case. He died a few months later.

Richard Helms, appearing before a congressional committee in 1975, said, "I have been in the government for thirty-two years. When you are finished, the only thing you have left is your reputation. If I do not have my reputation left when I leave the government, I have lost thirty-two years."

As I have made clear, Paul is not an admirer of Richard Helms. But he certainly agrees with what Helms had to say about reputation. Using the same yardstick, Paul lost thirty-six years. For when he retired, his reputation was still clouded and no real attempt had been made to remove the cloud. David Wise's excellent book *Molehunt* restores some of Paul's reputation, and he is grateful for that.

But when he retired, he knew there was no practical way to give him his reputation back other than a monetary settlement. He could think of no more obvious, explicit or positive way for CIA to admit that a mistake had been made, that he had been wrongly accused.

Paul still believes deeply in the work that CIA does and respects its accomplishments on behalf of the United States and the Western World. He considers himself fortunate to have been part of the Clandestine Service for more than twenty-five years. Now that he knows the truth, he believes that Angleton and the others were aberrations, not worthy of the high regard he has for the honorable men and women with whom he served.

13. Safe Harbor

W E ARRIVED in Tucson to begin a new life on the Fourth of July, 1978. We have lived in this house for almost fifteen years, a sharp contrast with the twenty-one houses we occupied over the last nineteen years before Paul retired. It is a comfortable home in a pleasant neighborhood, with much of our time spent outdoors. In our "golden years," it suits our needs perfectly.

Tucson is not a metropolis, far from it. It has been described as an overgrown cow town. We find that what we need is here, more or less, and we don't miss the Beltway or trying to get through Georgetown on M Street at high noon. Looking out on the mountains that ring this desert valley with the evening sun against them, I can think of nowhere else I'd rather be. Except perhaps New York City on a shopping trip. I must admit I miss that.

Many of the traditions of the Old West, cowboys, cattle ranches, the horse culture and Native Americans are still alive here. The border with Mexico lies a scant ninety miles south of us, and we have adopted the habit, followed by many of the early settler families, of taking off for Mexico for a quick change of scene when we want a little time off from Tucson.

I have done charity work since I was a teenager, and I worked for charity one way or another in each of the foreign countries in which we served. I am busy with it here. I find joy in this kind of work and feel rewarded in a way that nothing else can match.

We have made new friends, and they keep us busy with their generous hospitality, so our life is not dull. We have frequent visitors who come to reminisce and soak up the sunshine. Some are old friends from the Agency, and they keep us up to date on the rumor mill in Washington. Others come from as far away as Trinidad and Sweden, and they refresh our memories of the years we spent there.

Susan lives in McLean, not far from Langley headquarters. She has two fine sons, Jamie, who is fourteen, and Patrick, twelve. We travel east at least twice a year to visit. Paul has surprised everyone, including himself, by his devotion as a grandfather. We spend a summer vacation in California with Susan and the boys each year, and he forgoes golf, tennis, etc., to do what the boys want. My observation is, that since he is no longer working at a demanding job, he's able to give his grandsons more attention than he was ever able to give Susan.

Paul has kept himself busy. He tried six months of retirement, doing the gardening, tending the roses and trying his hand at Mr. Fixit, at which he is a disaster. He found all of that a terrible bore. So he looked around and found some things to do that interest him, including business and politics. He works about half a day, and tries to play golf or tennis the other half.

If Paul broods over what was done to him at a key time in his career, he's done a good job of concealing it from me. I honestly believe he's put all that behind him and interested himself in new endeavors and new people. He looks for something new to do every day. There are books out now that have set the record straight about what happened to him. The authors of these books have been out here to talk with him, as they have spoken with others, and Paul has been as open with them as his concept of need-to-know would allow. He has set only one condition on his willingness to talk—he does not want to be part of any CIA bashing. The authors have kept faith with him.

None of Paul's good friends would think of him as religious—certainly I never did. But I believe now that he survived his ordeal and came through whole because he had faith, faith in his country, faith in his God and faith in himself. He has a very special belief in a Supreme Being that has nothing to do with going to church on Sunday. He has built his own small temple of faith—he's never asked me in—and the flame that burns there has never even flickered. So I don't worry about Paul, he's on solid ground.

Paul says we are like a couple of tumbleweeds, blown this way and that by the winds of destiny. We have somehow managed to be places where important things were happening. Korea when the North Koreans invaded, Berlin at the height of the Cold War, Stockholm to receive an important Soviet naval officer defector, Moscow for Penkovskiy, etc.

Now we are rooted, and I find security and tranquility in that. I fall asleep to the sound of the desert wind whispering softly through the palm and eucalyptus trees that surround the house. I wake in the morning to the cries of the doves that are everywhere. Every now and then, thoughts come crowding in that I prefer not to deal with, so I pretend they are not there. I am at peace. I am content. Life goes on.